M000279945

Taste of Malta

Taste of Malta

Claudia M. Caruana

HIPPOCRENE BOOKS
New York

Throughout this book, Maltese characters are used in the titles only; in the text, Maltese words are in italics.

Early 19th century Maltese costumes by
Francesco Zimelli, *Raccolta di Costumi Maltesi,*
courtesy of the National Library of Malta

For information, address:
HIPPOCRENE BOOKS, INC.
171 Madison Avenue
New York, NY 10016

Library of Congress Cataloging-in-Publication Data
Caruana, Claudia M.
Taste of malta / Claudia M. Caruana.
p. cm.
Includes bibliographical references and index.
ISBN 0-7818-0524-4
1. Cookery, maltese I. Title.
TX723.5.M35C267 1997
641.59458'5—dc21 97-41257
CIP

Printed in the United States of America.

Dedicated to the memories of
my two grandmothers,
Glaudina Spiteri Consiglio
and
Antonia Lanzon Caruana
in whose kitchens I spent many happy hours.

The foods we eat and the ways in which we prepare them are among the strongest and most enduring expressions of our culture.

Peter Kaminsky

New York Times Book Reveiw, October 19, 1997

Contents

Acknowledgements

This book would not have been possible without the encouragement of my mother, Carmen, and father, John J. Caruana, who died as I was completing the manuscript. Others who have been instrumental in its development are my publisher and editor at Hippocrene Books, George Blagowidow and Carol Chitnis, respectively; Giom Grech; Grazio Falzon; Sandro Grima; Charles DeMicoli; Joseph Vella; Carmen Grech Polise; Victor DeBattista; Antoine Zammit; Michael Piscopo; Dan Carlinsky; Edward McCoyd; Gary Goldberg, The New School Culinary Arts Program; Barbara Ostmann; and Rich Rubin in the United States; Albert Vella, Bank of Valletta, Toronto; Michael Zarb; Alfred Grech; Wilfred and Rita Camilleri in Canada; Gemma Said, Esther Said, Gesters Restaurant, Xaghara; Tony and Anne Spiteri, *Ic-Cima* Restaurant, Xlendi Bay, Grace Farrugia; and Ludgard Gatt in Gozo; and Joseph Boffa, The National Library of Malta; Louisette Sant Manduca, The Fontanella Tea House Restaurant, Mdina, Tony Scerri, Bobbylands Restaurant, Dingli Cliffs, Joe and Liz Lanzon, Josephine Caruana, and Rosemary Grima in Malta.

A very special thank-you to Colman Andrews, editor of *Saveur* magazine, photographer Maura MacEvoy whose photograph of stewed rabbit appears on the cover, and her husband, Steven Wagner, both of whom traveled with me to Malta in 1995. A portion of this book first appeared in *Saveur* magazine, November/December 1995.

Also, a special thanks to the Malta National Tourist Office in New York City, the Maltese Center in Astoria, New York, and the Maltese community in Toronto.

And of course, I can't forget to mention my brother John and my nieces Gina, Jill, and Lindsay Caruana, all of whom have spent many hours in my kitchen.

It would not have been possible without all of you. *Nirringrazzjakom minn qalbi.* Thank you with all my heart.

In My Grandmothers' Kitchens

Although it no longer seems like yesterday, I remember vividly those mornings during the 1950s, sitting at the table in my Nanna Tona's Astoria, New York basement kitchen, where she would work miracles with pastry dough and ricotta. I'd marvel at her nimble hands rolling out dough at the counter for what seemed like hours.

At that time, it was of no concern to me that this was tedious work—I'd always think about *pastizzi*—fist-sized, flaky dough pockets with ricotta, peas, or chopped beef filling that made wonderful Sunday night snacks. That was the time when my aunts, uncles, great aunts and uncles, cousins, and other relatives, would get together.

While making the *pastizzi*, Nanna Tona would often reminisce about growing up in Malta. Malta, the largest of a string of five tiny islands in the Mediterranean, is 60 miles south of Sicily and 120 miles north of Tunis, with a land mass only four times the size of Manhattan. In this far-away place, my grandmother would make *pastizzi* and other traditional dishes such as *ravjul*, similar to ravioli, *aljotta*, a fish and garlic soup, *soppa tal-armla*, a vegetable soup, and *imqaret*, dates encased in pastry (which at the time I thought were *just awful*) for her widowed father and three younger brothers. She married my grandfather, Lawrence (Wenzu), when she was 16 and emigrated with him, my father, and Aunt Melita, to New York City several years later in the early 1920s.

My other grandmother, Nanna Glaudina, also emigrated from Malta at about the same time with my grandfather, Giuseppe (*Guz*). Unfortunately, she never seemed to have mastered Nanna Tona's knack for making *pastizzi*. Nanna Glaudina made *qassatat* instead. These also were ricotta-filled pockets, but the dough was not supposed to be flaky. A Maltese joke called *qassatat* "mistakes." No one seemed to care in our family: these "mistakes," were devoured just as quickly!

Qassatat are just a part of the fond food memories from the many family gatherings at Nanna Glaudina's house on Sundays. My parents, brother John, and I would arrive soon after Mass on Sunday mornings, just in time to help pour a large pot of meat sauce and ladle several cups of uncooked rice into a large, well-greased, oblong Pyrex dish. This was our favorite: *ross fil-forn*. Other Sundays, there might be *timpana*, a very filling dish of macaroni, meat, tomatoes, and eggs, encased in a pastry dough.

More often on Sundays, however, either my grandmother or mother would make *mqarrun fil-forn*—a very similar dish but without pastry crusts. The macaroni, usually penne, ziti, or rigatoni, was always blackened and crunchy on top. Like many children, my brother and I would always try to "sneak off" some of the blackened, crunchy parts when no one was looking. Never mind that our Nannu Guz noticed!

If a relative or family friend had been to Malta recently, chances were good that he or she brought *gbejniet*, small, dried sheep cheeselettes, sometimes plain, other times, coated with coarse, black pepper. Some Maltese families, then and now in North America, attempted to make their own fresh *gbejniet*, with varying success. Fresh *gbejniet* are solid and similar in size to more expensive goat cheese (cheveres) available in North America, Europe, and elsewhere, but much more moist and less crumbly. They also have a less "gamey" taste. In Malta, fresh *gbejniet* are often mashed and used in place of ricotta in several dishes. They often are served with soup, but you'll find people eating them at breakfast, and as appetizers and snacks, too.

My grandmother stored the dried *gbejniet* she received from friends in large Hellmann's mayonnaise jars kept on the top shelf of a cupboard. Sometimes, we would snack on the *gbejniet* or have them in a salad with fresh tomatoes; other times, my grandfather might grate the dried *gbejniet* in a small cheese grinder—the same way most people grated Parmesan cheese.

When either my brother or I visited during the week, Nanna Glaudina would prepare *froga*, an omelette with cold, thin spaghetti mixed with eggs and sometimes bits of ham and a hint of ground cumin. She would pan fry the mixture in olive oil until the bottom was browned and very crunchy. The spaghetti then was flipped over with a metal spatula so the other side could become crunchy, too. The *froga* would be served hot, with mounds of freshly grated Parmesan cheese.

And, there was rarely a summer day at home when we did not snack on *hobz biz-zejt*, crusty bread—usually Italian—drenched in olive oil, smeared with a crushed tomato, and seasoned with ground black pepper and salt. Often, we would top the *hobz biz-zejt* with capers, olives, or anchovies.

At the homes of many Maltese friends, there would be other traditional specialties such as stewed rabbit (*fenkata*) and pastry ribbons known as *xkunvata*.

As the daughter of a chef and a member of an immediate and extended family who enjoyed good food and celebrated Maltese tradition, I always believed that the food I ate at home, I would find everywhere when I visited Malta.

But almost twenty years later, soon after college in the mid-1970s when I made my first of several visits to Malta in search of my heritage—but not necessarily my relatives—I discovered that Maltese cuisine, with the exception of *pastizzi* sold as snacks, was difficult to find on restaurant menus. It was only then that I decided to visit relatives ... and never regretted that decision. They opened their hearts and kitchens to me and welcomed me to their tables.

There was a simple reason why Maltese cuisine infrequently appeared on restaurant menus then: Most Maltese families rarely dined out, and those who did, often did so with foreign business associates or friends whom they wrongly assumed would prefer international fare, not the authentic dishes created in their own kitchens.

Fortunately, that philosophy has changed. Several restaurants now specialize in Maltese cuisine; many are frequented by local residents and visitors, alike. (Some of my favorites in Malta, in addition to the restaurants that have provided several recipes for this collection, include Ta'Marija, Mosta, Ta' Kolina, Sliema, and It-Tokk, The Suncrest Hotel, Qawra.) What has not changed, however, is the tradition of what pleasurable eating is all about in Malta—freshly prepared, locally available food.

Today, Maltese families—wherever they live—continue to enjoy much of the same cuisine that their grandmothers, mothers, and aunts prepared, using many of the same ingredients in their own homes. In fact, if you ever have listen to a group of Maltese talking, after they discuss politics—which always seems to be on everyone's mind—don't be surprised if the conversation then changes to food. This even has been the case of a lively Malta Internet group whose Maltese and non-Maltese subscribers span the globe. They will write about the *pastizzi, gbejniet,* or the *fenkata, bigills,* and *lampuki* pie they remember their mothers or aunts making, or about where they might find a recipe for a specific dish. Then, there may be advice on where a difficult-to-locate ingredient such as mixed spice or treacle may be purchased. Others like to reminisce about their culinary experiences in Malta.

For example, Peter Pricetoe now retired and living in Yorkshire, England, noted: "As an English family living in Malta between the two World Wars, we were forbidden to eat any dairy produce because of undulant fever from the goats that were milked at the doorstep. In about 1936, however, a Maltese family invited us to their box at the Opera House and during the interval, *pastizzi* were brought round. Rules or not, we ate them from politeness and my father said that he felt like weeping for all the years he had denied himself the pleasure (actually Valletta, Floriana, and Sliema had by that time been declared 'closed areas' where the sale of raw goat's milk had been banned). Nowadays, when in Malta I eat my morning *pastizzi* at the La Valette Cafe opposite the ruins of that same Opera House and remember..."

For readers with Maltese backgrounds, I hope this collection of recipes will rekindle the memories of your childhood and our mothers, grandmothers, and aunts and sometimes our fathers, grandfathers, and uncles, too, who all were "custodians" of the family kitchen. But more important, I hope you will continue to savor and share our traditional cuisine with your family and friends. Do let me know about your favorites. I want to hear from you and would be happy to include your thoughts in a revised edition of this collection in the future.

For readers new to Maltese cuisine or those who have visited Malta and are interested in preparing some of the dishes that you may have sampled, I hope you will try many of the recipes in this collection and add several of them to your family's traditions. Let me know about your experiences!

Remember, no recipe is written in stone. Recipes change with time, families, and the availability of ingredients. Surely, our ancestors made substitutions, so feel free to improvise, too.

Malta, a tiny island nation that has withstood centuries of foreign domination, is prepared for the twenty-first century. Despite the proliferation of fast food chains and the hectic lifestyles of the Maltese, the traditional cuisine prepared by our grandmothers and great-grandmothers still reigns supreme in Malta . . . and in many cases, in our homes in North America and other places around the world, too.

—Claudia M. Caruana, January 1998

From My Kitchen to Yours

Nanna Glaudina, rest her soul, was fond of saying, *"Il-hajja tibda fil-kcina."* "Life begins in the kitchen." As a child, I wasn't quite sure what she meant. But as an adult who spent many hours in the kitchen—cooking, eating, and cleaning-up with my family and friends—I saw this to be the true family room.

The last thing a cookbook should be is intimidating, and I hope you will find this collection of recipes from my family and friends in the United States, Canada, and Malta to be a celebration of tradition, and a tribute to our heritage and good eating.

Modern home cooks, myself included, need to be mindful of health issues that were unknown to our grandparents and great-grandparents. In times past, having enough food to eat was crucial, so that many food choices that our ancestors made might not be appealing, appetizing, and may even be much less healthful by today's standards. To be certain, the emphasis on fresh fruits and vegetables and fish in traditional Maltese cuisine is healthy. But I believe my ancestors would forgive my modifying or suggesting changes in some of the less health-conscious traditional recipes.

A case in point are eggs. Many traditional Maltese recipes called for raw or undercooked eggs. Others use what seems like a large number of eggs in recipes compared to many of today's reduced fat recipes. For example, I've seen a traditional Maltese recipe for stuffed chicken in an old cookbook that used four uncooked eggs and two chopped hard-boiled eggs in the stuffing!

I have vivid memories of my Nannu Wenzu eating a bowl of raw eggs or sometimes eating as many as six fried or scrambled eggs at one sitting. And he wasn't the only relative or Maltese friend who consumed large quantities of eggs and lived to old age. It seems Sylvester Stallone's Rocky was not unique in seeing the potential of swallowing raw eggs!

But, seriously, for many people living on small islands like Malta where meat was both scarce and if available, expensive, eggs were an important and usually an inexpensive source of protein. It was no wonder then, that they would be used frequently.

When in Malta recently, I visited friends who would add a raw egg to the hot soup they fed their invalid mother every day at lunchtime. Mother had celebrated more than 90 birthdays!

Many modern Maltese cooks however, are becoming aware of the potential dangers of raw or undercooked eggs and no longer use them. Some home cooks will serve their families hard-boiled eggs instead, or may skip the eggs altogether. Many of the recipes presented here have been modified (I suggest that today's cooks consider reducing the number of eggs or substitute egg whites for whole eggs in many instances.) None of these recipes, however, have been tried with egg substitutes.

Kitchen Notes

Where I believe a specific recipe needs clarification or modifications to make it more health-friendly, I have included a section called ***Kitchen Notes***. Here, I include hints on how the recipe can be changed, how the dish might be used, special ingredients, or some history about its origins. Some examples:

- In Malta, what is most frequently referred to as minced meat (usually a combination of beef and pork chopped finely), throughout this book is called, "ground lean beef." Home cooks have the option of using pure beef or a combination of beef and pork. If ground pork is not available, consider using Italian sausage meat that has been removed from the casing. For cooks who prefer a "pork sausage taste" without the pork, try one of the special seasoning blends for pork found at gourmet shops or spice specialists such as Penzy's Spice House. When budgets were tight, many families would use canned corned beef instead of freshly ground meat.
- By North American taste standards, many Maltese dishes are "salty," due, in part, to commonly used ingredients—anchovies, capers, olives, Parmesan cheese—for example. Some Maltese cooks, like their American counterparts, add salt during cooking or use it at the table. In most cases, I have modified recipes to read: "salt and freshly ground pepper to taste," taking into account health concerns about limiting salt use. I personally do not add salt to dishes I prepare, and

many Maltese families living in Malta and North America are equally as conscientious about limiting their use of salt. I also suggest foods such as anchovies, capers, and olives be rinsed several times so their salt content is reduced. Also, check salt content labels of these ingredients; some brands have less salt.

- Recipe differences. Although Malta is a very small country, there are variations in ingredients used and the way specific dishes are prepared, sometimes village by village. There also are several Gozitan specialties. In researching this book, I learned about many of these variations and have included some of them in a section labeled, "Variations," after the recipe method is presented. Readers in North America probably remember a very successful telephone advertising campaign about two Italian sisters who didn't speak with each other because one's lasagna was better than the other's. Sometimes, we see the same emotions in Maltese families, too. Take, for example, my brother John and myself. There's always that friendly brother-sister argument about "who makes the best *mqarrun fil-forn.*" We try to let my nieces decide, but our mom usually gets the final word: my brother's *mqarrun fil-forn* is better!
- Tomato paste. Many traditional Maltese recipes call for tomato paste. The versatility of this low-cost ingredient may be unknown to some readers, but once you begin using it, you will become a devotee. Here's why: Tomato paste, plus fresh or canned tomatoes, can be the basis of some of the best sauces you'll ever taste. Using fresh ingredients with the tomato paste and tomatoes, you'll create the texture and taste you want and control both salt and fat content. Forget about the prepared jar sauces, which are often made with sugar or corn syrup, thickeners, and artificial ingredients. If you are in a pinch for time, a better option are canned sauces that do not have these objectionable ingredients. You can add your own herbs and spices. Be careful, however. Several brands may have either sugar or corn syrup as one of their ingredients.
- Olive oil. Many recipes call for olive oil, but as many Maltese cooks are quick to point out, when olive oil was too expensive for the family budget, they would use either an olive oil blend or another vegetable oil such as corn oil.
- Stock. Although many home cooks pressed for time choose to use canned broths, most are salty and laced with unfriendly, artificial

ingredients that have no place on your table; low-salt varieties tend to be tasteless and also have artificial ingredients. Frankly, there's no substitute for homemade stock. For cooks new to making stock, I've included recipes for vegetable, chicken, beef, and fish stocks that are easy-to-make and can be frozen for future use. Because you make them yourself, you can control both the salt and fat. I assure you, once you get in the habit of making your own stock (and soups, too), you'll consider those cans of stock in the supermarket history. Recipes for stock can be found in the Appendix, beginning on page 267.

- Garlic. Despite its many health benefits, garlic does not agree with everyone. Many of the recipes here use minced garlic. Of course, garlic can be eliminated altogether, but an alternative in many recipes that call for sautéing of onions and garlic in olive oil would be to leave the garlic whole and remove it after the sautéing step.
- Parmesan cheese. Forget about the "stuff" in the cardboard canisters found on the grocery shelf. Buy a wedge of Parmesan, Romano, or other grating cheese, grate it yourself and store it in a glass container in your refrigerator. You will notice the difference in taste from the "stuff" in the cardboard canisters.
- Herbs and seasonings. Whenever possible, purchase fresh herbs and seasonings from your green grocer or supermarket. Better still, grow your favorite herbs on your windowsill or in a small kitchen herb garden outside your home, if you have space.

I've created space for a small kitchen herb garden with several of the basics—basil, parsley, mint, marjoram, oregano, thyme, sage, and lemon balm. I snip leaves as I need them in the summer and early autumn. At season's end, I cut back the plants, dry the remaining leaves indoors, strip the leaves from the stems, and then store them in glass jars for use during the rest of the year.

I prefer my own dried herbs to most of those available in the supermarket, which can be of inferior quality (ground stems as well as leaves) and do not have "best if used by" dates on the labels. I have been pleased, however, with the quality of spices and herbs ordered from specialty mail-order companies and several of the gourmet (read: more expensive) brands.

If you choose to use dried herbs, remember they are more potent that fresh herbs, so reduce the amount used accordingly; otherwise, you will overpower the other flavors in the dish.

- Parsley is used in many Maltese recipes. I use the term, "Italian parsley," referring to flat-leafed parsley available at most green grocers. To maintain its flavor and color, add parsley later in the preparations of soups. Use curly parsley for garnish only. Use fresh parsley only; parsley flakes are tasteless.
- Mixed spice. This is a ready-made spice combination used frequently in Maltese cuisine. Ingredients vary from brand-to-brand, but usually are a blend of cinnamon, coriander, cassia, cloves, nutmeg, and ginger. There also are blends with caraway, fennel, and turmeric. Although you can blend these spices yourself, you may choose to purchase mixed spice. Most brands are blended in the United Kingdom (The British Pepper and Spice Co., Ltd., Lyons, and Schwartz) or Ireland (Goodall's), and several are available from mail-order sources found in the Resources section, pages, 279-293.
- Bottled water. Although many home cooks already use bottled water for cooking, it is essential for recipes that use yeast, baking enthusiast Sandro Grima says. "Tap water contains chlorine so it slows down the yeast. It will work, but bottled water will eliminate one risk which in yeast dough can make the difference between a loaf and a brick." Depending where you live, you may also choose to use bottled water instead of tap water for making stock, soups, and other dishes.
- Maltese bread. Several Maltese friends asked me if I would include a recipe for what many of us do not find in our homes in North America: Maltese bread. After considerable thought, many trials in my kitchen, and advice from Sandro, who makes Maltese bread using a sour dough starter obtained in Malta, I decided against it. Frankly, it is difficult to duplicate both the taste and texture of this wonderful bread in a home oven and with a sour dough starter that differs from the starter used in Malta.

As Sandro says: "Different starters can have drastically different rising/fermentation times so when one uses a new starter there is some experimentation to be done. For a recipe to be fool-proof, especially for a beginner, it has to be used in conjunction with a particular starter (or one with very similar properties). For example, the Maltese starter has a long rising period that helps develop taste. One of the most popular starters available in the United States rises at about four times the rate of the Maltese starter I have."

So, if you want to savor Maltese bread, you will have to make the trip to the Mediterranean or try one or more of the bakeries specializing in Maltese foods listed in the Resources section of the book, pages 279-293.

- Pre-baking bottom pie crusts. Although many home cooks like to skip this step when baking pies, results may not be optimum. Although using ceramic or metal weights placed over wax paper can help prevent shrinking during pre-baking of the bottom crust, the use of aluminum foil is also recommended. Several kitchen specialty stores and mail-order companies have products such as Pie Partner and others that can eliminate the need for ceramic or metal weights, wax paper, or aluminum foil. These products are often available through mail-order sources or at specialty kitchenware stores. A listing of specialty kitchenware mail-order sources is provided in the Resources section of the book, pages 279-293.
- Sugar. In many traditional dessert recipes, icing sugar is specified. This is the British name for confectioners' sugar.
- Parchment paper and rice paper are frequently recommended to line baking trays and dishes in several Maltese dessert recipes. This paper helps transfer doughs from one place to another and is invaluable when unmolding desserts from pans or cooking sheets. Common wax paper can be used in a pinch, but the results can be less than satisfactory.

As Nanna Glaudina was also fond of saying: *"Mhux boghod mid-dar jekk mhux boghod mill-kcina.* We are not very far from home if we are not very far from our kitchens."

As I am fond of saying: *"Merhba fil-kcina tieghi, u Sahha dejjem!* Welcome to my kitchen, and good health!"

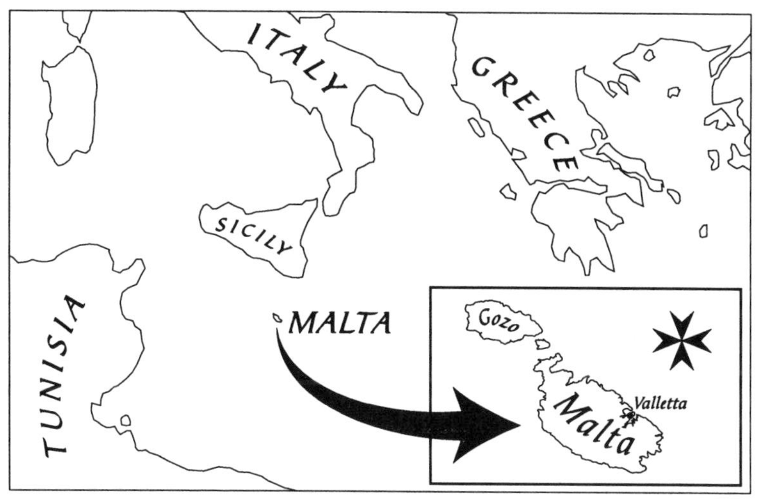

A History Bubbling with Intrigue

Because of their location—in the middle of the Mediterranean—the Maltese islands have played a role in history far larger than their size, a mere 122 square miles.

The islands were believed to have been first settled by inhabitants from Sicily as early as 4000 B.C. The Copper Age saw new arrivals, people who built massive Megalithic temples that pre-date England's Stonehenge. This civilization soon collapsed and was followed by the Bronze Age.

By the Ninth Century B.C., the Phoenicians found Malta hospitable for their trading activities and soon after, the Carthaginians arrived. The Romans took command in 218 B.C. and their occupation lasted more than 1,000 years. Other subsequent invaders included the Turks, Arabs, Spaniards, The Knights of St. John, later to be called the Knights of Malta, and even Napoleon Bonaparte, himself. He departed, however, after only seven days. Malta also earned the grim distinction of being the most bombed place in Europe during World War II while it was under British rule. Despite continual bombing by both the Italians and Germans and near starvation during the War, Malta did not surrender.

Not Quite the Knights in Shining Armor

The Knights of St. John have a special place in Maltese history because they cultivated the arts and built Valletta, the city that was to become Malta's capital. Many of the churches, St. John's Co-Cathedral for example, and great fortifications built during their rule, remain as unique examples from a baroque city.

Founded in 1085, the Knights of St. John were supposed to care for pilgrims who fell ill while visiting the Holy Land, which then was in Islamic hands. By the time the Crusaders captured Jerusalem in 1099, the Knights' role changed dramatically; they no longer provided medical care for ill pilgrims, but became defenders of Christianity.

After Jerusalem again changed hands in 1187, they were forced to leave for Acre. When it was taken over by the Arabs in 1291, the Knights were forced to move their operations to Cyprus. Rhodes became their new home in 1310 and for more than 200 years, they kept the Turks at bay in the eastern Mediterranean.

By 1522, the Knights where no longer welcome in Rhodes and were given Malta by Charles V, Emperor of Spain, in 1530 as a permanent home. They protected the Maltese from invaders and from the massive Turkish attack, The Great Siege, in 1565. Soon after, they began rebuilding the nation's fortifications.

But there was another side to the Knights. They lived luxuriously, buying houses, patronizing the arts, and keeping mistresses although they were supposed to be celibate.

My kingdom for a Falcon?

No, not quite. The Peregrine falcon, the prototype for the Maltese Falcon, now extinct in these islands, did breed on the cliffs near Ta' Cenc, Gozo. After the Knights were given the Maltese islands by Charles V, Emperor of Spain, they were required to provide him with a Peregrine falcon for rent every year on All Saints Day, November 1.

The Knights' reign came to an abrupt end in the late 1790s when Napoleon and the French landed in June 1798 and gave them four days to leave. The French plundered the Knights' homes, but were not long-term victors in Malta. They were kicked out by the British in 1800; the latter governed Malta until 1964 when the colony became independent.

A Gardjola, a typical look-out post overlooking Valletta. Most Gardjolas have an ear and an eye carved in stonework.

St. John's Co-Cathedral in Valletta was built between 1573 and 1577 during the reign of the French Grand Master La Cassiere on the plans of Maltese architect Girolamo Cassar. (Both photos courtesy of the Malta National Tourist Organization.)

The Malta-America Connection

While much has been written about Malta's close cultural ties with mainland Europe, particularly Sicily, and its ceaseless exposure to Arab and Turkish territorial infringements which went on well into the nineteenth century, when marauding for slaves and other bounty finally came to an end, less, however, has been written about Malta's relationship with the United States.

Several highlights of the Maltese-American connection, according to Paul Cassar, M.D., and described by Joseph Vella, include:

- In the early 1750s, a Maltese master craftsman John Pass (an Anglicized version of his Maltese surname Pace) helped recast the Liberty Bell after it cracked. A faded painting of Pace, posing around the bell with other artisans, showed a tattoo on his arm with a Maltese design.
- Benjamin Franklin sent Knights of Malta Grand Master Emanuel de Rohan a commemorative medallion in honor of America's newly won independence from British rule under King George III in 1783. During the conflict, a small contingent of Knights joined the French Navy in support of America's revolt.
- The first American Consul to Malta was appointed in 1796, making it possible for American warships to anchor in Malta for supplies during the Tripolitan War, 1801-1805. For the duration of the conflict, Malta was committed to the American cause.
- During the War of 1812 between England and the United States, Malta served as a British naval bastion against units of the American Navy. But by 1842, the United States and Great Britain agreed to maintain a balanced presence of naval armed forces in the Mediterranean. It was the start of a long partnership between the two navies, which still endures.
- The American Navy decided to make Malta a station for its warships in 1847, when for its own use, Spain took over Port Mahon, on the island of Minorca, from the Americans.
- As unlikely as it may seem, both Malta and the United States have at one time ruled the same country. The Knights acquired St. Croix in 1653, with several other adjoining small islands; it was sold to Denmark in 1733, and purchased by the United States in 1916.
- New Orleans, Louisiana, then a French colony, saw the earliest Maltese migration to the new world in 1780. By 1818, other Maltese followed in larger numbers, and by 1855, at least 100 had settled in the United States. Mass Maltese emigration to America coincided with the discharge of skilled artisans from the Maltese dockyard in 1919, at the conclusion

of World War I. Many found work in the automobile manufacturing industry centered around Detroit, Michigan, while others settled in the northeast, particularly metropolitan New York. A large contingent of Maltese also settled in and around San Francisco. There also was mass emigration to other countries, notably Australia and Canada, at this time.

- Malta was one of the staging areas for the U.S. Armed Forces' invasion of Sicily during World War II. Both General Dwight D. Eisenhower and President Franklin D. Roosevelt visited Malta. FDR paid tribute to the Maltese people for their valorous service to the allied war effort by presenting a plaque on December 8th, 1943. It read, in part: "In the name of the people of the United States of America I salute the island of Malta. Its people and defenders. . . have rendered valorous service far and beyond the call of duty." The President's message concluded with: "What was done in this island maintains the highest traditions of gallant men and women who from the beginning of time have lived and died to preserve civilization for all mankind."
- Another large wave of Maltese emigration occurred soon after World War II, with many Maltese beginning new lives in the United States, Canada, and Australia.
- Today, there are arguably as many native born Maltese, or nationals of Maltese origin living abroad, as there are Maltese living in Malta.

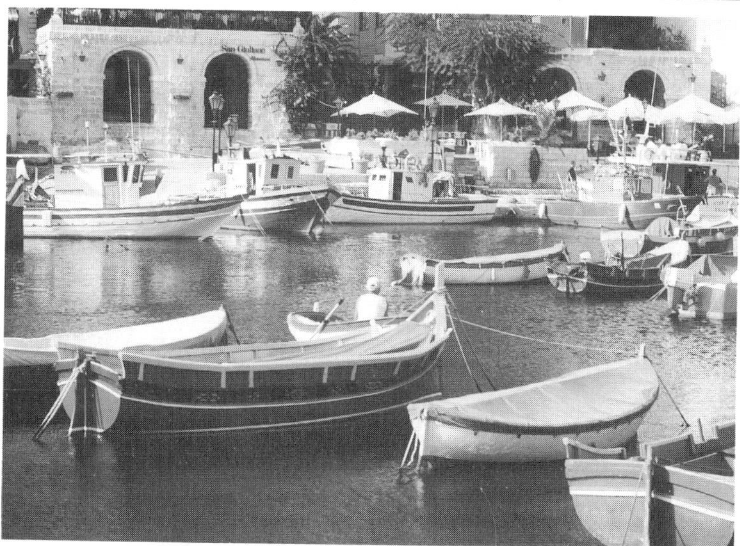

St. Julian's Bay, Malta. (Photograph by Claudia M. Caruana)

Chapter 1

Maltese Cuisine Yesterday and Today

Maltese Cuisine Yesterday and Today

Like her mother, aunts, and grandmothers before her, Maria Cassar is busy in her kitchen on Sunday morning after Mass, preparing for the family's dinner.

She carefully places a pork roast, neatly surrounded by sliced potatoes and thinly sliced onions, in an aluminum roasting pan. She places a tea cloth over the roast, leaves her flat, and hurries along the dusty streets of Qormi (pronounced Ormee), to 10 Triq St. Katerina (St. Catherine Street).

The elderly woman, dressed in black, stops in front of a side-opening garage door that, from the outside, is indistinguishable from the others on the block. I see her inside, at Lucy DeBono's bakery, where she and other men and women, clutching heavy pans and casserole dishes with *timpana* or *ross fil-forn,* will have their families' dinners roasted or baked. Later in the day, they, or other family members, will return to pick up the cooked entrées, ready for serving. The cost for using the services of a community baker: usually, a little more than $1.

Country wisdom says that Malta's best bakers hail from Qormi, which since its earliest days in the 1400s was referred to as *Casal Fornaro,* the Baker's village, because of its many bakeries. Less than 10 miles from Malta's capital, Valletta, Qormi, a crowded city of nearly 15,000 residents, is a maze of confusing, narrow streets. It is also well-known for its centuries-old carved doorways and balconies—now, unfortunately, in varying stages of decay.

The following day around noontime on Malta's sister island Gozo, I am speaking in faltering Maltese to a handful of women, a few with fidgeting small children, gathered in Grace Farrugia's bakery in Nadur. Not surprisingly, their English is better than my Maltese so our conversation crosses two languages.

Here, several women are waiting to pick up freshly baked *pastizzi,* the hand-sized, flaky-pastry pockets filled with either ricotta or peas and minced meat or *qassatat,* similarly filled but with a less flaky dough, which they prepared earlier. Others come to purchase loaves of crusty bread. Grace, herself, is preparing what look like small pizzas layered with fresh tomatoes, peppers, and *gbejniet*. Several small, whole fish topped the *ftira* I saw Grace making that morning.

The women ask about my family, and I tell them how much being here today reminds me of home in New York, especially when my Maltese grandmothers, Glaudina and Tona, were alive and prepared many of the same dishes. Pleased that my grandmothers shared with me their cooking secrets, they ask how I make specific dishes, especially after I say my father is a retired chef. I feel as if I have known these women all my life. Perhaps I have.

To modern cooks with well-equipped kitchens, a community baker or bakery appears anachronistic. Maltese women, like their counterparts in other industrialized countries, do have modern kitchens equipped with stoves and ovens.

But the visits to community bakers have as much to do with convenience—the absence of grease-laden ovens and a cool kitchen during blistering hot summer days—as they do with tradition and getting together with friends and neighbors.

In earlier times, it was impractical to have individual ovens in crowded living quarters, so Maltese women would take their family's meals for roasting and baking to the large, wood-burning, brick ovens the town's bakers used for bread making. Foods needing slow simmering, such as soups and stews, were placed in earthenware and heated on stone hearths called *kenurs*. Consequently, many Maltese foods were simmered slowly.

My friend Michael Zarb, now living in Canada, remembers earlier times in Malta when homes did not have ovens and were dependent on taking items that needed to be baked to the bread baker on Sundays. "The first home oven that I remember was a tinbox with a door at the front and a hole in the bottom, a contraption that was placed on the *spiritiera tal-ftila* or wick stove, to heat it."

To this day, many of the community bakers in Malta and Gozo continue to use wood-burning ovens and fuel them with scraps of wood, even twigs and newspapers. This fuel is often provided by their customers or neighborhood children.

A flare for using what is available

Few would question the notion that cuisine is integral to a nation's identity and contributes to its color, charm, and vitality. Like the country itself, Maltese cuisine is a study in contrasts—and quirky. It is a non-homogeneous blend of tradition, improvised during the ages, using what was locally available.

Understandably, the inhabitants of any island quickly learn to work with what they have, and the Maltese are masters of ingenuity in this regard. Although much of traditional Maltese cuisine is simple, it should not be dismissed as "peasant food." This cuisine celebrates the fruits, vegetables, herbs, and spices that can be cultivated on the island's poor, arid soil—or grow there wild—rather than exotic ingredients. Local vegetation includes broad beans (favas), peas, cauliflower, pumpkin, squash, kohlrabi, tomatoes, potatoes, peppers, eggplant, onions, garlic, olives, figs, prickly pears, dates, almonds, carob, and wild mint, thyme, dill, and capers. Maltese onions and potatoes are exported to other countries in Europe.

Produce not imported from neighboring Europe or North Africa is grown on small family-owned farms, set back and hidden by rubble walls in the more rural and less-populous Gozo. This smaller island, a few miles northwest of Malta across the Fliegu Channel, is often referred to as the island of farmers and fishermen, the principal occupations of its residents for many centuries.

Comino, (*Kemmuna*) the one square mile island nestled between Gozo and Malta, was named for the spice cumin, which once grew wild there. Today, Comino popular with day excursioners, is home to a handful of year-round residents, a police station, church, and a seasonal hotel. There are also two other uninhabited islands: Filfa and Comminotto (*Kemmunett*).

The "influence" of long-ago visitors

There is little doubt that traditional Maltese cuisine—like the Maltese language—is the result of the country's checkered history of invasions and occupations. Malta's desirable location—coupled with its excellent natural harbors—has made it especially attractive to those groups determined to dominate and control the Mediterranean. "Visitors," welcomed and unwelcome, have included the Phoenicians, Romans, Carthaginians, Arabs, Normans, Turks, Italians, Knights of St. John, French, and the British. Each contributed to the culture and the cuisine; for example, the Italians, the Sicilians in particular, introduced several pasta dishes such as *timpana, lasagna,* or *ravjul* plus scrumptious pastries like *kannoli*; the Arabs brought, *mqaret,* fried date cakes and *kusksu,* a soup with fava beans, peas, and pasta. *Pastizzi,* the pastry snack, was believed to have originated with the Turks but also is similar to the cheesecakes called "*sfogliorati*" found in Calabria, Italy. Many of the vegetable, meat, and fish pies, no doubt, were introduced by the British who occupied Malta for many years.

But many historians believe the Knights perhaps had the most culinary influences on Maltese cuisine.

The Order, presided over by a Grand Master, was divided into eight Langues—Provence, Auvergne, France, Italy, Argon, Castile, England, and Germany. The Langues had individual houses or Auberges, several of which remain and have been restored in Malta's capital, Valletta.

Each of the Auberges would have its own chef, often from the country of origin, who undoubtedly prepared favorite dishes from home and made arrangements for importing meat and exotic ingredients. Maltese assistants, working in their kitchens, probably shared Maltese cuisine with the chefs, based on the locally available fruits, vegetables, and wild rabbit. It was also during this time that Maltese sauce, more commonly known as Maltaise sauce, was believed to have been created. Maltaise sauce has the same ingredients of the typical hollandaise sauce—butter, egg yolks, and lemon juice—but also makes use of orange juice and grated orange rind. Like hollandaise sauce, Maltaise Sauce is used as a topping on vegetables. The Knights were also credited for encouraging the Maltese to cultivate potatoes and onions in the valleys of their small islands.

But there was another side to the Knights' interest in cuisine. In *A Taste of History: The Foods of the Knights of Malta,* author Pamela Parkinson-Large provides a glimpse of the exotic meals the Knights would have served their guests: flamingo, baked swan, or roasted head of wild boar, all of which were imported. From all historical accounts, however, the Maltese shunned these extravagances and preferred what was locally available.

Bounty from the earth

By virtue of the islands' size and location, meat must be imported to Malta. So with good reason, then, meat is used infrequently—Sunday dinner—or sparingly in many traditional dishes. Therefore, it is not difficult to understand how other foods like fruits, vegetables, and pasta played an important role in Maltese cuisine.

Vegetables—artichokes, eggplant, peppers, marrows—typically are stuffed with bread crumbs, rice, or ground meat, and herbs, such as marjoram, mint, thyme, and oregano. Like their neighbors in Italy, the Maltese enjoy *barbuljata*: scrambled eggs, tomatoes, and grated cheese. In the summer, *Kapunata,* fried tomatoes, green peppers, eggplant, onion, with garlic, mint, capers, and oregano is popular, and sometimes eaten sandwich-style.

Although there are small groceries and the equivalent of green grocers, many Maltese women prefer to buy their vegetables, fruits, and herbs, and haggle about prices from vegetable vans (*tal-haxix*) perilously parked on Malta's narrow streets. Until recently, both farmers and fishmongers would alert potential customers of their presence by clashing pans and yelling, *Hut!* (Fish!) or *Haxix!* (Vegetables!) in the streets at daybreak. Pity the family members who enjoyed sleeping late!

But in addition to the fruits and vegetables they purchase or grow themselves, you'll see many Maltese picking figs (*tin*) or three varieties of prickly pears (*bajtar tax-xewk*), when in season, from neglected trees and bushes along the roadside.

Gathering wild herbs such as thyme, mint, dill, and borage, and capers, which grow unabashedly in rural areas in crevices and crannies almost everywhere, is a popular Sunday family activity in the summer. The capers are pickled in vinegar at home and stored in large jars for year-round use. If you bristle at the thought of the brine-tasting capers sold commercially, you will be very pleased with the capers available in Malta. Many Maltese also like to pickle small onions in vinegar (*basal tal-pikles*) until they turn brown. These are used year-round, either as a stand-alone appetizer or with other dishes.

The island of "the rabbit"

Because meat had to be imported, it was characteristically absent from most meals or used sparingly except for Sunday dinners. Remembers Michael Zarb: "At home, we didn't need the Church to prohibit meat on Friday, we barely ate meat once a week on Sundays. Usually it was a pork roast with the *patata fil-forn* (oven roasted potatoes) or '*kapuljat* (chopped meat) with the *ross fil-forn* (baked rice) or *mqarrun fil-forn* (baked macaroni). For a special feast day, it might be a *fenek* (rabbit) or *serduq* (hen)."

In earlier times, Malta was populated by wild rabbits, but that is not the case today. Rabbits are raised by farmers or by individuals for their own families. Rabbit, *fenek*, is grilled, fried, or simmered in stew with wine and tomatoes and served with spaghetti, pasta, or sometimes rice.

"Come for *Fenkata*," Maltese people often tell their friends. While *fenkata* means rabbit stew, "the suffix, *-ata*, adds a happy metaphorical plus emotional seasoning to the national dish, my friend, Grazio Falzon, notes. Some people call it feasting and celebrating on rabbit, another friend says.

"In my mind," Grazio says, "*fenkata* brings instantly fond and happy memories of partying at St. Thomas Bay. On Sundays, we used to bike or walk from Zejtun to the Bay. We would spend the day there swimming, and at noon Karmni would serve this scrumptious rabbit stew at her shack-like diner. Now that was a *Fenkata!* My God, my neurons can almost recreate the smell, the taste, the happiness of those *fenkata* parties."

An estimated two million rabbits were bred in Malta in 1995, making the Maltese the highest consumers of rabbit meat per capita. Rabbit breeding is so efficient in Malta that several other countries are looking into the methods used by the Maltese to improve their rabbit breeding programs.

Another passion of many Maltese are game birds such as pigeon (beccun), which are raised by individuals on their rooftops. Traditionally, pigeons are stewed or made into pies. On Sundays in Valletta, the capital, there is a large open-air market selling pigeons for breeding. . . . in addition to all the typical and traditional items one might expect to find: clothing, food, and crafts.

Quail and other game birds, when available, also are welcome on many Maltese tables.

Pork or veal roasts are eaten on Sunday when families traditionally get together. The meat usually is seasoned with local herbs and spices, surrounded by thinly sliced potatoes and onions, and then roasted either at home or at a community bakery.

Warm up to soup

Soups also are important in traditional Maltese cuisine. In late spring when the broad or fava bean is available, a hearty soup called *kusksu* is popular. Like an Arab dish with a similar name, this soup has favas with onion, tomato purée, and small-tube pasta. Fresh cheese such as *gbejniet* can be added at the time of serving. *Soppa tal-armla*, widow's soup, was so named because it was inexpensive to make, and uses seasonal vegetables like kohlrabi or cauliflower with a raw egg, added at the time of serving the hot soup. Although the practice of adding a raw egg to hot soup is declining, it still exists in some Maltese homes. Some families will serve a hard-boiled egg with the soup instead.

Eggs have always served as an important source of protein in Malta and they are used in large quantities in several dishes, although a generation of more health-conscious cooks is preparing these dishes with fewer eggs today.

Aljotta, a garlicky soup with tomatoes, potatoes, onions, marjoram, mint and seasonal fish, is enjoyed year-round. Marrows, onion, carrots, and celery are ingredients in lighter soups called *brodus*. Maltese *minestra* is similar to Italian minestrone, but usually contains pumpkin and pasta as well. *Kawlata* is similar to *minestra*, but is flavored with a piece of ham or pork bone.

Come for the lampuki

Local fishermen supply the island with a variety of fish year-round. Because fish takes the place of meat in many Maltese homes, it is served often and in a variety of ways: grilled, in stews and sauces, pies, and in soup. Sauces are kept simple to accentuate the fish, and might include tomatoes, garlic, capers, mint, and a dash of vinegar. A favorite is *hut biz-zalza*, seasonal fish in season served in a sauce of tomatoes and capers.

The variety of fish available in Malta is largest in summer months and includes bass, grouper, pilot fish, amberjack, white bream, swordfish, trill, and dentex. Always popular is *qarnita*—octopus—used in stews or cooked and served cold in salads. The Maltese also have a passion for *rizzi*, sea urchins, which they slice open with a sharp knife and eat raw. If you visit many of the seaside villages, you'll often see divers bringing up the *rizzi.*

Just as rabbit might be considered a national dish in Malta, so is *lampuki* or the dorado fish. Filling for *lampuki* pie—*torta tal-lampuki* includes fried and deboned *lampuki,* onions, cauliflower, spinach, tomatoes, olives, and usually raisins. It is not unusual for many returning Maltese-Americans, -Canadians, and -Australians to time their visits home to savor the *lampuki,* usually from late August to early November.

But Maltese in metropolitan New York who are unable to return for the *lampuki* season, can still savor *lampuki* if they visit the Greek community in nearby Astoria. Several Greek stores in this community have *lampuki* shipped by air in September and October. Of course, orders for the *lampuki* must be placed weeks in advance.

After the rains subside in late September, snails appear in large numbers throughout the Maltese countryside. Families collect them for appetizers and stews. Often, snails are eaten cold or with a sauce of fresh herbs that includes parsley and garlic.

Always time for a pasta dish

Pasta dishes, which are frequently reheated and served the following day, are basic to Maltese cuisine and culture. Best known are *timpana,* a deep-dish macaroni, chopped meat, and hard-boiled eggs entrée encased with a pastry crust, and *ross fil-forn,* baked rice, traditionally prepared and served at Sunday dinner. *Mqarrun fil-forn,* baked macaroni minus the crust, *injokki mimlija* (stuffed pasta shells such as manicotti) and lasagna, very similar to the Italian dish, are also popular. *Ravjul,* dumplings filled with ricotta and fresh, minced Italian parsley, similar to Italian ravioli, are a popular Friday dish. For a quick meal there is *froga tal-ghagin*—leftover spaghetti mixed with eggs and bits of ham, sprinkled with cumin and then pan-fried to a crisp in olive oil. Equally easy to prepare is *tarja,* thin spaghetti mixed with ricotta and melted butter.

Bread—the soul of Maltese cuisine

Bread always had an important place on the Maltese table, and even the Knights, in a quest for control when they arrived, took over all bakeries on the island. They later rescinded this very unpopular decision.

Maltese bread—*hobza*—with a sour dough taste has a crisp crust and is shaped in round loaves indented by a knife. One side, often partially blackened, is sometimes higher and darker than the other. Baked directly on the oven's bottom, it is a part of all meals and also a favorite snack. The best known snack is *Hobz biz-zejt*—olive oil-soaked bread, smeared with crushed tomatoes (in summer) or tomato paste when fresh tomatoes are unavailable in winter. This is seasoned with coarsely ground black pepper, salt, and frequently capers or anchovies. Observant visitors will see workers eating *hobz biz zejt* or another traditional Maltese bread *ftira*, a flat, partially risen round loaf with a hole at its center at lunchtime. The *ftira* will often be stuffed with tomato and a piece of cheese, usually a *gbejna*, plus a drizzle of olive oil. Even stale bread has a place on the Maltese table. Sandro Grima, for example, said his family always cubed their stale bread, deep fried it in olive oil, and then used it as croutons in soup. Similarly, thinly sliced stale Maltese bread is also deep fried in olive oil and eaten with soup by many families.

Dairy products are not emphasized in Maltese cuisine with the exception of ricotta and *gbejniet*. The latter are individual goat or sheep milk cheeselettes, formed in half-dollar size containers, and traditionally made in Gozo. In earlier days, the containers were bamboo; today, they are made out of plastic.

There are three kinds of *gbejniet*—*gbejna friska* (soft, moist, fresh cheeselette), *gbejna moxxi* (a dried cheeselette), and *gbejna tal-bzar* (a dried cheeselette heavily coated with black pepper). On many Gozotian rooftops, you can see rows of homemade *gbejniet* drying in special, open-air boxes, called meat lockers, resembling bird cages.

Gbejniet friski are added to soups like widow's soup, *soppa tal-armla*, at the table. When a recipe calls for ricotta, *gbejniet friska* often are substituted in Malta. *Gbejniet moxxi* can be grated and used in place of Parmesan cheese, as my grandfather used to do. These cheeses are also served as an appetizer or as a dessert. They frequently are placed on an appetizer table and eaten with *galletti*, traditional Maltese crackers made with semolina.

The Maltese sometimes jokingly refer to Gozitans as *gbejniet*—an American equivalent to calling someone a "cheese head." But the

Gozitans are always quick to point out there is only one place where *gbejniet* are eaten more frequently than on Gozo—that is Malta, of course!

St. John's Breadfruit

The carob or St. John's Breadfruit tree, native to Malta, flourishes with grace during the hot summer. Usually in October or November, the brown pods are picked from the trees' twisted trunks. Now, these pods are used for fodder, but in days past, they were eaten during difficult times. During World War II, carob pods were roasted and ground; the grounds were used as a coffee substitute. Hard candy, traditionally sold on Good Friday, *karamelli tal-harrub*, is made from syrup extracted from the dried pulp. The syrup, *Gulepp tal-harrub*, is a well-known cough and cold remedy available in Maltese pharmacies.

Nectar of the Gods

Honey produced on Gozo and Malta is light amber with much of its flavor and fragrance resulting from the islands' wild thistle, clover, and thyme, from early May through August. During the winter months, the honey produced has a hint of orange, when the blood orange tree is in bloom.

Beekeeping in Malta and other Mediterranean islands goes back centuries. During the Roman occupation, Malta was referred to as *Melita*, the Latin name for "honey." Then, honey-making was strictly controlled by the government and anyone caught pilfering honey could be put to death. Melita remains a popular girl's name in Malta.

Sweets/Desserts

Fresh fruit is always welcome for dessert in Malta. In the spring, there are strawberries (*frawli*), and later on, melons (*bettih*), peaches (*hawh*), apricots (*berquq*), nectarines (*nuciperski*), and grapes (*gheneb*). In the autumn, there are pomegranates (*rummien*) and red and yellow medlars (*naspli*), similar to apples.

Blood oranges, very sweet oranges with deep red flesh, are available around the Christmas season and are similar to those found in neighboring Sicily and other Mediterranean countries. Tangerines also are available at this time of year.

But the Maltese have a passion for sweets, too, many of which are seasonal or linked with religious holidays, festas or festivals. The exception, perhaps, are the *pastizzi*, the pastry encased pockets of cheese or peas/ham, available almost everywhere and eaten both as snacks and as desserts.

Available year round are *kannoli ta' l-irkotta*, similar to Italian cannoli, except that ricotta and candied fruit are used for the filling and *Imqaret*, fried date cakes flavored with anise and essences of orange or tangerine.

Biskuttini tal-Maghmudija, christening biscuits flavored with anise and decorated with pastel icing, are served at baptismal parties and at other times. *Biskuttini tal-lewz*, macaroons, also are popular.

Sahha—Maltese for "To Your Health"

Although Maltese wine-making dates back to Roman times, numerous occupations, especially by the Arabs, squelched interest in cultivating this art. Local wine-making did flourish again with the arrival of the Knights, who were fond of the grape and imported wine from their originating countries. Although the Knights were credited with several improvements—insisting that the grapes be grown closer to the ground with leaves covering the grapes to prevent the scorching sun from drying them out and shielding them from the violent winds with rubble walls—the wine-making industry has always been small. In addition to factors such as poor soil, arid weather, and difficulty in harvesting, there are no central grape growing areas on either island.

Two local vintners, Marsovin and Lachyrma Vitis, do produce several white and red table wines from Maltese grapes, and also process imported Italian grapes for some of their wines.

Despite the islands' miniscule size, there is a national soft drink, *Kinnie*, and three liqueurs, *Tamakari, Madlien, and Batjra*. Flavored with oranges, aromatics, and bitter herbs, the *Kinnie* formula is a well-guarded secret, like Coca-Cola. Typically, *Kinnie* is drunk ice cold and served with a slice of orange or lemon. A diet version of *Kinnie* also is available. In locations where *Kinnie* is not distributed, try a similar beverage, Sanpellegrino's *Chinnoto*, made in Italy and frequently available in Italian groceries and specialty stores.

Tamakari, the Maltese after-dinner liqueur, is made with six natural herbal extracts, which to my taste is similar to Bénédictine, the liqueur named after the Benedictine monks at the Abby of Fecamp in Normandy, France. Although it was originally called Empire Liqueur when first produced in the late 1920s in the town of Qormi, the name *Tamakari* has its roots in the family name of the liqueur's developers: the family was known as *Ta' Makari*, meaning, "of Makari." *Tamakari* continues to be produced in the same Qormi plant.

Madlien is an herbal liqueur and *Batjra* is made from prickly pears. There also are two locally produced beers—Hop Leaf and Cisk Lager.

And coffee after dinner? The Maltese like to flavor theirs with a sprinkle of grated cloves.

Chapter 2

Appetizers and Snacks

Antipasti u Ikel Ħafif

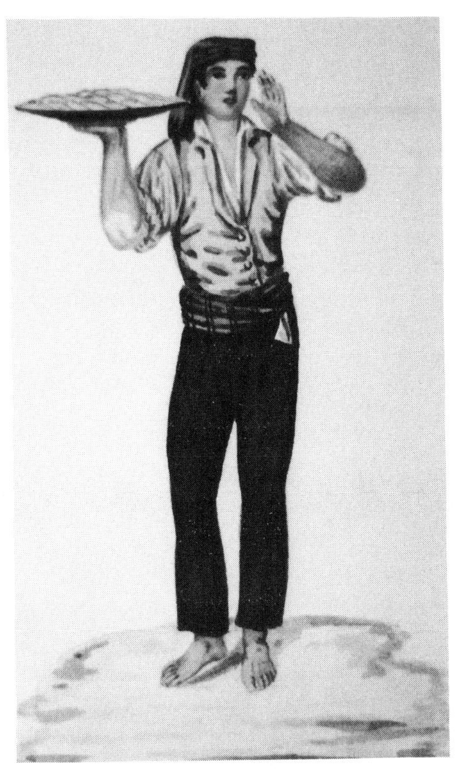

Maltese Pizza

Ftira

My nieces affectionately call this "Maltese pizza," although there are many pizzerias in Malta serving what is typically Italian pizza. I have very fond memories of watching Grace Farrugia in her Nadur, Gozo bakery carefully preparing this Ftira, reminiscent of pizza, for several of her customers.

Ingredients

1 pound fresh pizza dough (thawed frozen dough can be substituted if fresh dough is unavailable; the results are less predictable, however)
3 large potatoes, peeled and very thinly sliced
1 large onion, very thinly sliced
2 large tomatoes, very thinly sliced
2 tablespoons capers, drained and well-rinsed
½ cup black olives, pitted and sliced
2 or 3 *gbejniet* or other cheeselettes
1 can (2 ounces) flat anchovies, drained and well-rinsed
or 1 can bristling sardines (optional)
1 teaspoon chopped fresh oregano
5 tablespoons olive oil

Method

Preheat the oven to 400°F.

On a well-floured hard surface, use a rolling pin to carefully roll out pizza dough, making certain to roll in one direction only. Carefully fold dough in half, and transfer dough to pizza pie plate. Unfold and stretch into place. Carefully cover dough with the potato slices. Place onion slices over the layer of potatoes and then add tomatoes. Garnish with capers, olives, cheese, and anchovies. Sprinkle oregano over top and drizzle with olive oil. Bake for approximately 40 minutes until crust is golden.

Serve piping hot.

3 to 4 servings.

Variations

For a quick *ftira* "pizza," especially for a crowd of young people or children, consider using pocketless pitas, often found in groceries carrying Greek products. They are different from the regular pitas used in many Middle Eastern recipes. Olive oil can be drizzled on pocketless pitas after all the ingredients have been neatly arranged. Bake for approximately 25 minutes in a greased casserole dish or pie plate, and serve hot.

Kitchen Notes

Maltese home cooks use sliced small tomatoes, larger than plum tomatoes, to make *ftira*.

Oven bricks that can be placed directly under pizza, available in kitchen specialty stores and the kitchen goods departments of many major department stores, help distribute heat more evenly and usually result in better crusts for breads, pizzas, and other baked goods.

Broad Bean Paste

Bigilla

Many older Maltese have fond memories of the "Bigilla Man," a hawker who would sell hot bigilla on wintery nights in the small towns and villages of both Malta and Gozo. Today, bigilla often is served as an appetizer or a spread for bread or Maltese crackers, galletti.

Ingredients

2 pounds fresh favas, shelled, or two cans (8 ounces each) of favas, well rinsed and drained, or one jar (16 ounces) shelled favas, or 1½ pounds dried fava beans
2 tablespoons baking soda (only if using dried favas)
4 to 6 cloves garlic, peeled and chopped
2 to 3 sprigs Italian parsley, minced
2 tablespoons capers, well rinsed and drained
1 chili or hot pepper, seeded and chopped (dried hot pepper can be substituted or 1 tablespoon hot sauce such as Tabasco)
3 to 4 tablespoons olive oil
several sprigs fresh mint for garnish
salt and freshly ground pepper
loaf of crusty bread

Method

For dried favas:

In a large bowl, soak washed beans and 1 tablespoon baking soda in water for 48 hours. Change water and add another tablespoon of baking soda after 24 hours. Rinse thoroughly. Peel and remove skins. Rinse beans again and proceed as follows as with fresh or canned favas.

For fresh or canned Favas:

Simmer peeled favas until soft, approximately 20 minutes. Drain and rinse cooked beans thoroughly. Grind (on pulse setting) in blender or food processor beans, garlic, Italian parsley, capers, hot sauce or fresh chili, and olive oil until smooth. Serve in dessert-size bowl. Garnish with sprigs of fresh mint. Season with salt and pepper to taste.

Can be served with crusty bread or crackers, either hot or chilled, although many Maltese prefer this dish hot.

Kitchen Notes

Carefully check cans that read, "fava beans/ful medames." Often, these ful are brown broad beans. These beans are quite good, but are not the same favas described in this and other recipes throughout this book.

Fresh fava beans, like peas and lima beans, freeze well. Select small pods that are not bulging with big beans at your green grocer when the beans are in season, usually in spring. Remove the beans from the pods and place them in plastic bags or storage containers. When a recipe calls for them, I'll pop them out of the freezer, rinse thoroughly, and use them as I would fresh favas, just increasing cooking time slightly.

Bigilla freezes well so you might want to consider this option.

For a different taste, I add a few cilantro leaves in the blender when preparing the *bigilla* instead of the hot pepper.

Special Health Note

A severe and sometimes fatal allergy to fava beans can occur in susceptible people. This allergy is often genetically based. If you have never eaten fava beans, eat only a small quantity at first to make certain you do not have this allergy.

Lenten Bread

Ftira tar-Randan

Although it is a sweet, Ftira tar-Randan, which can be served with sugar instead of honey, was traditionally made and eaten in Gozo during the Lenten season because it used no animal fats. But notes one Maltese friend, his mother made this treat, called "sfinga," often, "not only during Lent ('Randan' in Maltese, 'Ramadan' in Arabic)." He believes that perhaps the "less poor ate it only during 'Randan' while for the poorer ones, it wasn't only 'Randan' fare. I wouldn't call it 'popular food' in a modern sense, rather a sweet treat easily supplied at home. We couldn't afford to indulge in bought sweets, a situation which was very common with many people in those days, the twenties, thirties, and forties, during the war, and times of poverty."

Irrespective of its origins, ftira-tar-randan is a great treat.

Ingredients

15 ounces fresh, unleavened bread dough at room temperature (can be purchased from a bakery)
2 tablespoons olive or other vegetable oil for each slice
4 teaspoons honey or 4 teaspoons confectioners' sugar

Method

Cut bread dough in six large slices. Roll out each slice on a well-floured marble surface until the dough is very thin. Heat oil in a large skillet. Fry each piece of dough on both sides until brown and crispy. Remove from skillet and drain on absorbent paper. Drizzle with honey or sprinkle with sugar.

Serve warm.

4 to 6 servings.

Lima Bean and Chick Pea Salad

Insalata tal-Fażola u Ċiċri

This is one of the simplest, yet most popular, quick meals enjoyed by Maltese people, especially in the summer months. It is easy to prepare and can be extremely appetizing. The salad is eaten with crusty bread, spread with tomato paste and dipped in olive oil. It is not unusual to complete the meal with anchovies, olives, canned tuna, and fresh tomatoes.

Ingredients

1 pound fresh lima beans, shelled or one can (16 ounces) lima beans
1 pound dried chickpeas (soaked for several hours and drained) or one ready-to-use can (19 ounces) chick peas
2 to 5 cloves garlic, peeled and crushed
2 sprigs Italian parsley, chopped
2 sprigs fresh mint, chopped
approximately 10 large olives, drained, well-rinsed, and sliced
2 tablespoons tomato paste
4 tablespoons olive or other vegetable oil
salt and freshly ground pepper
one loaf crusty bread

Method

In a large bowl, toss the lima beans and chick peas. Add crushed garlic, parsley, mint, olives, and tomato paste. Drizzle olive oil and mix again. Season to taste with salt and pepper.

Serve cold with crusty bread.

3 to 4 servings.

Capunata (Ratatouille)

Kapunata

Ingredients

1 to 2 large onions, peeled and chopped
2 to 4 cloves garlic, peeled and minced
4 tablespoons olive or other vegetable oil
1 large eggplant, peeled, sliced, and chopped (see Kitchen Notes)
4 large ripe tomatoes, peeled and chopped
2 green peppers, seeded and sliced
1 cup pitted olives, well rinsed, drained, and sliced
3 tablespoons capers, well rinsed and drained
1 to 2 sprigs fresh Italian parsley
1 sprig fresh oregano
1 sprig fresh mint
salt and freshly ground pepper
2 cups vegetable stock
2 cups cold water
loaf crusty bread

Method

In a large skillet, sauté onions and garlic in olive oil until onion becomes translucent, usually between 5 and 10 minutes. Add eggplant, tomatoes, and peppers, and sauté for another 10 minutes. Add olives, capers, parsley, oregano, mint, and salt and pepper to taste. Cover with stock and water. Simmer until all vegetables are tender, approximately 20 minutes, turning them over, when necessary. Add water if the liquid begins to dry out.

Serve warm with crusty bread.

4 servings.

Kitchen Notes

To reduce the natural bitterness of eggplant, soak eggplant slices in cold, salted water (Kosher salt is best for this) for approximately 15 minutes. Rinse thoroughly and then continue with the recipe.

Some cooks prefer using basil instead of mint.

While ***kapunata*** is frequently served as an appetizer with either Maltese crackers (*galletti*) or crusty bread, this also makes for a wonderful vegetarian entrée. It is also often served with grilled fish.

Fried Spaghetti

Froġa tal-Għagin

In the Caruana household, this dish was often served with a simple salad as a Saturday lunch. It's a snap to make with leftover spaghetti and was one of the first dishes both my brother and I learned to make when we were still children. My teenage nieces' friends call this "Maltese fried spaghetti," but to us, it always will be froga.

Ingredients

1 pound cold, cooked thin spaghetti such as spaghettini or angel hair, which should be broken in half before cooking
2 eggs, well beaten
4 ounces diced ham (optional)
1 teaspoon cumin seeds, crushed (optional)
2 sprigs Italian parsley, minced
salt and freshly ground pepper
4 to 8 tablespoons olive or other vegetable oil suitable for frying
3 tablespoons freshly grated Parmesan cheese
curly parsley for garnish

Method

In a large bowl, mix thoroughly cold, cooked spaghetti and eggs. Add diced ham and crushed cumin and parsley. Season with salt and pepper to taste. Divide spaghetti mixture into four equal portions. Heat olive oil in small skillet. When hot, add one-quarter of the spaghetti mixture. Lower heat. As spaghetti on the bottom becomes golden and crunchy, gently turn over with a spatula so the top also browns and become crunchy, approximately 10 to 15 minutes. Drain on absorbent paper towels. Repeat for the other portions.

Serve immediately with freshly grated Parmesan cheese and garnish with parsley.

4 servings.

Kitchen Notes

Some home cooks prefer to add the grated Parmesan cheese to the spaghetti mixture before cooking. Either way, this is an extremely satisfying dish.

Vermicelli Omelette

Froġa tat-Tarja

This is another version of the recipe above that many Maltese friends also enjoy.

Ingredients

1 pound cold, cooked thin spaghetti (such as angel hair) which should be broken in half before cooking
1 cup whole-milk or part-skim ricotta
2 eggs, well beaten
3 to 4 tablespoons freshly grated Parmesan cheese, divided
2 cups tomato sauce or 2 ounces tomato paste and 1½ cups cold water (sauce or water should be chilled)
1 to 3 sprigs Italian parsley, minced (optional)
salt and freshly ground pepper
4 to 8 tablespoons olive or other vegetable oil suitable for frying
curly parsley for garnish

Method

In a large bowl, mix thoroughly spaghetti, ricotta, eggs, and one-half of grated cheese until smooth. Add tomato sauce, minced parsley, and salt and pepper to taste. Mix well. Divide mixture into four portions. Heat olive oil in small skillet. When hot, add a portion spaghetti mixture. Lower heat. As spaghetti on the bottom becomes golden, gently turn over with a spatula so the top also browns and becomes crunchy, approximately 10 to 15 minutes. Drain on absorbent paper towels. Repeat for the other portions. Garnish with curly parsley.

Serve immediately with remaining Parmesan cheese.

4 servings.

Angel Hair with Butter and Ricotta

Tarja bil-Butir u l-Irkotta

This is another one of those simple recipes that Maltese friends remember fondly. In Malta, tarja refers to a very thin spaghetti, similar to angel hair or spaghettini.

Ingredients

1 pound freshly cooked thin spaghetti that has been broken in half, such as angel hair, or spagettini, drained, and warm
2 cups whole-milk or skim-milk ricotta
1 stick unsalted butter or margarine
1 to 2 sprigs Italian parsley, minced (optional)
freshly grated Parmesan cheese
salt and freshly ground pepper

Method

Place cooked spaghetti in large sauce pot over low heat. Add ricotta, butter, parsley, Parmesan cheese, and salt and pepper to taste. Mix thoroughly while the saucepot is on low heat. The butter should be completely melted, usually in less than five minutes before serving.

Serve piping hot with a salad or fresh cheeselettes.

4 servings.

Kitchen Notes

It is not unusual for some Maltese families to substitute another type of pasta for the spaghetti.

Bread and Oil (Open Tomato Sandwiches)

Ħobż biż-Żejt

When the first tomatoes are ready in my home garden, we celebrate with hobz biz zejt. Although our family sometimes makes hobz biz zejt from store-bought tomatoes in the winter, nothing is quite the same as those summer tomatoes for this snack. When tomatoes are not available, a smear of tomato paste can be substituted, but not, in my opinion, with the same results.

Ingredients

1 large loaf crusty bread (such as peasant or rustic bread)
3 large ripe tomatoes, each cut in half
olive oil for dunking
salt and freshly ground pepper

Method

Cut bread into large, thick slices. Set aside. Pour olive oil in flat-bottomed bowl. Dip individual slices of bread in olive oil. Rub sliced tomato against the oil-dipped bread so they are well-smeared with tomato. Season to taste with salt and pepper.

3 to 4 servings.

Variations

At noontime in Malta, it is not unusual to see many worker eat *hobz biz-zejt*, made with *ftira*, the partially proofed flat bread with the hole in the center. A combination of sliced olives, anchovies, capers, and garlic are often placed on top of the smeared tomato on olive oil in either the *ftira* or crusty bread slices alone. *Gbejniet* are often eaten with *hobz biz-zejt* either as a topping or as an accompaniment. Still another variation: topping the *hobz biz-zejt* with either fresh, tender fava beans or fresh chick-peas. The latter is a favorite with my friend Victor Debattista.

Sun-dried Tomatoes with Olive Oil

Ħobż biż-Żejt u t-Tadam

On hot summer days in Gozo, it isn't unusual to see slices of crusty Maltese bread soaked with olive oil and topped with tomatoes drying on netting. It's also done in the gardens of Maltese families in North America, sometimes on a barbeque grill or in aluminium plates or trays. You can imagine the interesting conversation it creates when friends are visiting for a summer afternoon barbecue! Here's how Giom Grech makes this treat.

Ingredients

1 large loaf crusty bread, sliced thinly
olive oil
2 to 3 medium-size ripe tomatoes, sliced thinly (plum tomatoes usually work best)
salt and freshly ground pepper

Method

On a sunny, hot day, prepare netting, using four stakes. A grill or disposable aluminum trays also can be used. Thoroughly soak individual pieces of crusty bread in olive oil. Place tomato slices on top of the bread. Carefully place oil-soaked bread on netting, grill, or on aluminum trays and keep in direct sun at least five hours. The tomatoes should be at least partially dried when you are ready to serve the bread. Add salt and pepper to taste.

3 to 4 servings.

Kitchen Notes

The plastic netting that farmers and gardeners use to prevent birds from foraging their crops available in either hardware stores or garden supply shops, works well for making this backyard treat.

Maltese Scrambled Eggs

Barbuljata

Ingredients

1 large onion, peeled and diced
2 to 3 large ripe tomatoes, seeded and chopped
1 large green pepper, seeded and chopped
1 to 2 slices bacon, shredded (optional)
2 tablespoons olive or other vegetable oil
4 to 6 eggs, well-beaten (consider substituting 4 eggs plus 4 egg whites)
2 to 3 sprigs Italian parsley, minced
salt and freshly ground pepper
2 tablespoons unsalted butter or margarine
freshly grated Parmesan cheese, for topping

Method

In a large skillet, sauté onion, tomatoes, green pepper, and shredded bacon in olive oil, until the onion becomes translucent, usually between 5 to 10 minutes. Drain off and discard excess fat. Set aside. In a large bowl, mix eggs, parsley, and salt and pepper to taste. Pour the egg mixture and butter over the ingredients in the skillet and cover over low heat, stirring constantly, until the eggs have set, similar to making scrambled eggs.

Serve piping hot with Parmesan cheese.

4 servings.

Variations

Some Maltese families will use a small amount of chopped meat in place of the bacon when making this.

Stuffed Tomatoes

Tadam Mimli

Ah, for those hazy days of summer and all those fresh garden tomatoes. Here's another way to enjoy them, the Maltese way!

Ingredients

4 large, ripe tomatoes (tops removed and inside scooped out, chopped and held in reserve)
4 ounces unseasoned bread crumbs
1 to 2 hard-boiled eggs, shelled and chopped
1 to 2 teaspoons capers, drained and well rinsed
2 tablespoons pitted black olives, drained, well-rinsed, and sliced
1 to 2 sprigs fresh mint, minced
1 to 2 sprigs Italian parsley, minced
salt and freshly ground pepper
2 to 3 tablespoons olive oil
1 to 2 tablespoons red wine vinegar
juice from ½ fresh lemon
freshly grated Parmesan cheese

Method

In a medium-size bowl, toss tomato pulp, bread crumbs, hard-boiled eggs, capers, olives, mint, parsley, and salt and pepper to taste. Drizzle with olive oil, vinegar, and lemon juice. Toss again. Carefully stuff individual tomatoes with mixture. Sprinkle Parmesan cheese on top of the mixture. Refrigerate for at least two hours until ready to serve.

Serve cold.

4 servings.

Variations

Cold, cooked white rice can be substituted for the bread crumbs. The contents of a 6-ounce can of flaked tuna fish can also be used in place of the bread crumbs.

Maltese Cheesecakes

Pastizzi

This recipe is adapted from Wilfred Camilleri.

Ingredients

For the filling:

2 pounds whole-milk or part-skim ricotta cheese
2 eggs, well beaten
3 to 4 sprigs Italian parsley, minced
salt and freshly ground pepper

For the pastry:

One recipe *pastizzi* dough, page 276

Method

Preheat the oven to 400°F.

For the filling:

Mix the ricotta with the eggs, until smooth. Add parsley, and salt and pepper to taste, and mix again. Set aside.

For assembling the pastizzi:

On a well-floured marble board or other hard surface, roll out *pastizzi* dough as thin as possible. With a biscuit or pastry cutter, cut the dough into three- to four-inch circles. Put one tablespoon of the ricotta mixture in the middle of each circle. Fold each circle from the top and the bottom to the center and squeeze the edges together so that the pocket is sealed (the horizontal ends should be formed into points). Place individual *pastizzi* on an ungreased baking sheet. Bake for between 45 minutes and 1 hour or until the *pastizzi* turn golden brown.

You may need to experiment with the oven temperature and the cooking time. The *pastizzi* will be a golden-brown when ready. Serve warm with either coffee or tea, although they are great with an icy glass of *Kinnie* with a slice of orange or Sanpellegrino's *Chinotto.*

Makes 12 to 18 *pastizzi.*

Kitchen Notes

For home cooks short on time, consider substituting professionally made flaky pastry dough sometimes available from a local bakery. In Malta, many home cooks, female and male alike, find it too time-consuming and tedious today to make *pastizzi* at home. So it is not unusual for many people to purchase frozen *pastizzi* dough from neighborhood bakers to eliminate the most difficult step in their preparation. But many more will buy *pastizzi* at the bakery or from the various stands that sell them.

In a pinch, consider puff pastry doughs made by Pillsbury, Pepperidge Farm, or anyone else, available in the freezer section of many supermarkets in the United States or Canada.

Meat Pastizzi

Pastizzi tal-Laħam

This was the way I remember Nanna Caruana making meat pastizzi.

Ingredients

For the filling:

1 large onion, peeled and minced
1 clove garlic, peeled and minced
2 tablespoons olive or other vegetable oil
1 pound lean ground beef (a combination of beef and pork or ground pork can be substituted)
2 tablespoons tomato paste
3 large sprigs parsley, minced
salt and freshly ground pepper
1 cup cold water or beef stock
1 cup freshly shelled or frozen peas

For the pastry:

One recipe *pastizzi* dough, page 276

Method

Preheat the oven to 400°F.

For the filling:

In a large skillet, sauté onion and garlic in olive oil until the onion becomes translucent, usually between 5 and 10 minutes. Add ground beef and continue to simmer until the meat is no longer pink. Remove from heat. Drain off and discard excess fat. Return to heat. Add tomato paste, parsley, and salt and pepper to taste. Cover with water or stock. Simmer for another 15 to 20 minutes. Mix well and then add the peas. Simmer for another 10 to 15 minutes or until the peas are soft. Remove from heat.

Assembling the pastizzi:

On a well-floured marble board or other hard surface, roll out *pastizzi* dough as thin as possible. With a biscuit or pastry cutter, cut the dough into three- to four-inch circles. Put one tablespoon of the meat mixture in the middle of each circle. Fold each circle from the top and the bottom to the center and squeeze the edges together so that the pocket is sealed (the horizontal ends should be formed into points). Place *pastizzi* on a well-greased and floured baking sheet. Bake for approximately 45 minutes to one hour or until the *pastizzi* turn golden brown.

Serve piping hot.

Makes 12 to 18 *pastizzi.*

Pastizzi with Peas

Pastizzi tal-Piżelli

Ingredients

For the filling:

1 large onion, peeled and minced
1 to 2 cloves garlic, peeled and minced
2 tablespoons olive or other vegetable oil
2 tablespoons tomato paste
1 can (12 ounces) corned beef, flaked
3 to 4 sprigs parsley, minced
salt and freshly ground pepper
1 cup cold water
1 cup freshly shelled or frozen peas

For the pastry:

One recipe *pastizzi* dough, page 276

Method

Preheat the oven to 400°F.

For the filling:

In a large skillet, sauté onion and garlic in olive oil until onion becomes translucent, usually 5 to 10 minutes. Add tomato paste, corned beef, parsley, and salt and pepper to taste. Cover with water. Simmer for another 15 to 20 minutes. Mix well. Add peas. Simmer for another 5 to 10 minutes, until peas are very tender. Remove from heat. Cool.

Assembling the *pastizzi*:

On a well-floured marble board or other hard surface, roll out *pastizzi* dough as thin as possible. With a biscuit or pastry cutter, cut the dough into three- to four-inch circles. Put one tablespoon of the meat mixture in the middle of each circle. Fold each circle from the top and the bottom to the center and squeeze the edges together so that the pocket is sealed (the horizontal ends should be formed into points). Bake *pastizzi* on an ungreased baking sheet for approximately 45 minutes to one hour or until they become golden brown.

Serve piping hot.

Makes 12 to 18 *pastizzi.*

Cheese Qassatat

Qassatat bil-Ġobon

Ingredients

For the filling:

2 pounds whole-milk or part-skim ricotta cheese
2 eggs, well beaten
3 to 4 sprigs Italian parsley, minced
salt and freshly ground pepper

For the pastry:

One recipe for *qassatat* dough 1 or 2, page 274

Method

Preheat the oven at 400°F.

For the filling:

Mix the ricotta with the eggs, until smooth. Add parsley, and salt and pepper to taste, and mix again. Set aside.

Assembling the qassatat:

On a well-floured marble board or other hard surface, roll out *qassatat* dough as thin as possible.

With a biscuit or pastry cutter, cut the dough into three- to four-inch circles. Put one tablespoon of the ricotta mixture in the middle of each circle. Gather the edges toward the center, leaving it uncovered over the filling. Place *qassatat* on a well-greased and floured baking sheet. Bake for approximately 45 minutes to one hour, or until the *qassatat* turn golden.

Serve the *qassatat* either warm or cold, although most people prefer them warm.

Makes 12 to 18 *qassatat.*

Cheese Qassatat with Fava Beans

Qassatat bil-ful

Ingredients

For the filling:

2 pounds whole-milk or part-skim ricotta cheese
2 eggs, well beaten
3 to 4 sprigs Italian parsley, minced
salt and freshly ground pepper
1 cup freshly shelled, tender fava beans

For the pastry:

One recipe *qassatat* dough 1 or 2, page 274

Method

Preheat the oven at 400°F.

For the filling:

Mix the ricotta with the eggs, until smooth. Add parsley, salt and pepper to taste, and mix again. Gently mix in fava beans. Set aside.

Assembling the *qassatat*:

On a well-floured marble board or other hard surface, roll out *qassatat* dough as thin as possible.

With a biscuit or pastry cutter, cut the dough into three- to four-inch circles. Put one tablespoon of the ricotta mixture in the middle of each circle. Gather the edges toward the center, leaving it uncovered over the filling. Place *qassatat* on a well-greased and floured baking sheet. Bake for approximately 45 minutes to one hour, until the *qassatat* turn golden brown.

Serve the *qassatat* either warm or cold, although most people prefer them warm.

Makes 12 to 18 *qassatat*.

Qassatat with Anchovies

Qassatat ta' l-In'ova

A family favorite with the Grimas in Malta and the United States, this recipe was provided by Rosemary Grima who lives in San Gwann, Malta. In her home, she says, these qassatat disappear quickly!

Ingredients

For the filling:

3 large onions, peeled and minced
2 tablespoons olive oil
4 tablespoons cold water
1½ tablespoons tomato paste
5 ounces black olives, kalamata or similar (pitted and chopped)
6 anchovy fillets, drained, well-rinsed, and chopped
1 teaspoon mixed spice
salt and freshly ground pepper
2 pounds spinach, stems removed, chopped, and steamed
8 ounces cooked split peas

For the pastry:

One recipe for *qassatat* dough 1 or 2, p. 274

Method

Preheat the oven at 400°F.

In a large skillet, sauté onions in olive oil until onion become translucent, usually between 5 and 10 minutes. Add water, tomato paste, olives, anchovies, mixed spice, and salt and pepper to taste. Cook on low heat for approximately 10 minutes. Remove from heat. Add spinach and peas. Mix well.

Assembling the qassatat:

On a well-floured marble board or other hard surface, roll out *qassatat* dough as thin as possible.

With a biscuit or pastry cutter, cut the dough into three- to four-inch circles. Put one tablespoon of the anchovy mixture in the middle of each circle. Gather the edges toward the center, leaving it uncovered over the filling. Place *qassatat* on a well-greased and floured baking sheet. Bake for approximately 45 minutes to one hour, or until the *qassatat* turn golden brown.

Serve the *qassatat* either warm or cold, although most people prefer them warm.

Makes 12 to 18 *qassatat.*

Potato Qassatat with Favas

Qassatat bil-Ful u l-Patata

The first time I had these, I was visiting Ic-Cima Restaurant in Xlendi Bay, Gozo. I asked for the recipe and usually make them in spring when fava beans are small, tender, and in season.

Ingredients

For the filling:

4 to 5 large potatoes, peeled, chopped, boiled, and chilled
2 to 3 tablespoons unsalted butter or margarine
salt and freshly ground pepper
1 egg, well beaten
1 cup small, tender, shelled, uncooked fava beans

For the pastry:

One recipe for *qassatat* dough 1 or 2, p. 274

Method

With a hand beater or an electric beater, beat potatoes with butter, and salt and pepper to taste in large bowl. Add egg. Beat until smooth. Gently mix in uncooked fava beans. Set aside.

Assembling the *qassatat*:

On a well-floured marble board or other hard surface, roll out *qassatat* dough as thin as possible.

With a biscuit or pastry cutter, cut the dough into three- to four-inch circles. Put one tablespoon of the potato mixture in the middle of each circle. Gather the edges toward the center, leaving it uncovered over the filling. Place *qassatat* on a well-greased and floured baking sheet. Bake for approximately 45 minutes to one hour, or until the *qassatat* turn golden brown.

Serve *qassatat* either warm or cold, although most people prefer them warm.

Makes 12 to 18 *qassatat.*

Ricotta, Tomato, and Olives Salad

Insalata ta' l-Irkotta, Tadam, u Żebbuġ

Whenever I make this quick salad in summer, I wish I had fresh gbejniet. But the ricotta can be quite pleasant, too.

Ingredients

3 tablespoons capers, drained and well-rinsed
6 tablespoons olives, drained, well-rinsed, and chopped
1 jar (3½ ounces) or 1 can (2½ ounces) anchovies, drained, well-rinsed, and chopped
2 to 3 shallots, peeled and minced
1 to 2 cloves garlic, peeled and crushed
1 to 3 sprigs mint, minced
2 to 3 sprigs Italian parsley, minced
freshly ground pepper
olive oil
vinegar
3 to 4 large, ripe tomatoes, sliced
2 to 3 hard-boiled eggs, shelled and sliced
1 to 2 cucumbers, peeled and sliced
ricotta cheese, for topping

Method

In large bowl, combine capers, olives, anchovies, shallots, garlic, mint, parsley, and pepper to taste. Mix well. Drizzle with olive oil and vinegar. Set aside.

On a platter, arrange tomato, egg, and cucumber slices. In the center of the platter, place the salad ingredients.

Serve salad in individual bowls. Add ricotta at the table.

4 servings.

Peppered Cheeselettes and Tomatoes

Ġbejniet tal-Bżar u t-Tadam

I always look forward to receiving several packages of gbejniet bil-bzar when friends return from Malta or Canada (where they also are available from the Malta Bake Shop in Toronto.) I try saving them for summer salads with home grown tomatoes and shallots, which bring back memories of the simple yet elegant salads I so fondly remember eating in friends' homes in Gozo.

Ingredients

2 large shallots, peeled and minced (a red or yellow onion can be substituted)
1 to 2 cloves garlic, minced (optional)
2 tablespoons capers, drained and well rinsed
approximately 10 black olives, drained, well rinsed, and sliced
1 to 2 sprigs marjoram, minced
olive oil and vinegar for dressing
3 large ripe tomatoes, sliced
3 or 4 peppered cheeselettes (*gbejniet tal-bzar*), halved. (Other small, peppered cheeses can be substituted.)
1 cucumber, peeled and sliced (optional)

Method

In a large salad bowl, toss shallots, garlic, capers, olives, and marjoram. Drizzle with oil and vinegar. Set aside. Around the rim of a platter, alternate slices of tomato, cheeselettes, and cucumber. Place salad mixture in the middle.

Serve well chilled with additional salad dressing.

3 to 4 servings.

Chapter 3

Soups

Sopop

Widow's Soup

Soppa ta' l-Armla

The ingredients of this traditional soup, which has several variations depending on what village you're from in Malta and what vegetables are in season, are inexpensive although cooks today would find that difficult to believe with the high cost of fresh vegetables. The soup is usually made with a combination of white and green vegetables although some families will use carrots.

Ingredients

2 large onions, peeled and chopped
1 to 2 leeks, cleaned and chopped (optional)
2 tablespoons olive or other vegetable oil
3 large potatoes, peeled and sliced
1 head cabbage, washed, sliced, and shredded
1 cauliflower, stems removed, chopped
salt and freshly ground pepper
8 cups cold water
4 cups vegetable stock
3 to 4 eggs
gbejniet or cheeselettes, for topping
ricotta, for topping

Method

In large kettle or stockpot, sauté onions and leeks in olive oil until the onions become translucent, usually between 8 to 10 minutes. Add potatoes, cabbage, cauliflower, and salt and pepper to taste. Cover with water and stock. Bring to a boil and then simmer for 45 minutes to one hour, until the vegetables are tender. Bring to a boil again. Crack each egg into a small bowl, then carefully spoon into the soup. Cover and continue cooking until eggs are cooked throughly. Remove from heat. Ladle soup into soup bowls, making sure an egg is placed in each bowl.

Serve with fresh *gbejniet*, cheeselettes, or knobs of ricotta, which can be placed in each bowl.

6 to 8 servings.

Kitchen Notes

In some Maltese homes, either shredded lettuce or endives would also be used in this soup.

Poor Man's Soup

Soppa tar-Raġel Fqir

This recipe, which many believe may have originated among impoverished Maltese families who could not afford the ingredients of Soppa tal-armla, is very satisfying, says Carmen Grech Polise, who likes its simplicity.

Ingredients

4 to 5 cups cold water
1 large onion, peeled and chopped
½ head cauliflower, stems removed, cut in pieces
3 large potatoes, peeled and cubed
3 tablespoons tomato paste
2 to 4 tablespoons olive or other vegetable oil
salt and freshly ground pepper
1 cup fresh or frozen peas
2 to 3 eggs
loaf of crusty bread

Method

Put water in a large kettle or stockpot. Add onion, cauliflower, potatoes, and tomato paste. Drizzle with olive oil. Add salt and pepper to taste. Cook, covered, over medium heat, until cauliflower and potatoes start to soften, approximately 45 minutes to one hour. Add peas. Crack each egg into a small bowl, then spoon into the simmering soup. Cover and continue cooking until eggs are cooked throughly.

Serve immediately with a loaf of fresh, crusty bread.

3 to 4 servings.

Minestrone

Minestra

Ingredients

Vegetables in season, usually including

2 large onions, peeled and chopped
1 to 2 cloves garlic, peeled and minced
2 tablespoons olive or other vegetable oil
1 large pumpkin, scooped out, seeded, and sliced
3 large carrots, peeled, and sliced
1 courgette squash, peeled and sliced (another squash variety can be substituted)
½ head cabbage, shredded
2 large potatoes, peeled, and chopped
2 kohlrabi, peeled and sliced (a medium-size turnip can be used instead)
1 to 2 stalks celery, sliced
2 tablespoons tomato paste
2 to 3 sprigs Italian parsley, minced
1 large bay leaf
salt and freshly ground pepper
2 cups vegetable stock
10 cups cold water
½ cup uncooked, small pasta or rice
freshly grated Parmesan cheese for topping
loaf of crusty bread

Method

In large stockpot, sauté onions and garlic in olive oil until the onion becomes translucent, usually between 5 and 10 minutes. Add pumpkin, carrots, squash, cabbage, potatoes, kohlrabi, celery, tomato paste, parsley, bay leaf, and salt and pepper to taste. Cover with stock and water. Simmer until all vegetables are tender, approximately 60 minutes. The soup should be thick, almost like a stew. Add uncooked pasta or rice and more water if necessary. Simmer again until the pasta or rice is tender. Remove bay leaf before serving. Ladle into individual bowls.

Serve piping hot, adding freshly grated Parmesan cheese at the table. Served with a loaf of crusty bread, this makes for a very satisfying meal.

6 to 8 servings.

Variations

Some Maltese families will prepare this soup with beans either alone or in addition to the pasta or rice. Canned beans, such as chick-peas or kidney beans that have been drained and well rinsed, work well. Add them toward the end of cooking.

Vegetable Soup with Tripe

Minestra bil-Kirxa

Prepare *minestra* according to above recipe. Add approximately one pound of well cleaned tripe, that has been separately boiled for between one and two hours, to the *minestra* at the conclusion of cooking. Mix well.

Serve piping hot with a loaf of crusty bread.

6 to 8 servings.

Pork and Vegetable Soup

Kawlata

Prepare *minestra* according to recipe on p. 76, adding a pork bone during cooking. In some families, pork sausages are added toward the final 30 to 45 minutes of simmering, instead of the pork or ham bone. Unlike *minestra*, however, *kawlata* is not served with pasta or cheese.

6 to 8 servings.

Kusksu Pasta with Fava Beans

Kusksu bil-Ful

Ingredients

2 large onions, peeled and chopped
1 to 2 cloves garlic, peeled and chopped
2 tablespoons olive or other vegetable oil
2 tablespoons tomato paste
1 pound freshly shelled fava beans
1 pound freshly shelled or frozen peas
salt and freshly ground pepper
10 cups cold water
2 cups vegetable, beef, or chicken stock
1 cup *kusksu* pasta
freshly grated Parmesan cheese
loaf of crusty bread

Method

In large stockpot, sauté onion and garlic in olive oil until the onion becomes translucent, usually between 5 and 10 minutes. Add tomato paste, beans, peas, and salt and pepper to taste. Cover with water and stock. Bring to a boil and then simmer until the vegetables are tender. Bring to a boil again, add pasta and cook for between 10 and 15 minutes until the pasta is *al dente.* This should be a thick soup. Ladle into soup bowls.

Serve piping hot. Add freshly grated Parmesan cheese at the table. Served with a crusty loaf of bread, this can be a very satisfying meal.

6 to 8 servings.

Kitchen Notes

Do not confuse the pasta used in this soup with couscous, a traditional Middle Eastern dish. In Malta, Kuskus are very small pasta tubes similar to *acini di pepe* pasta found in Italian groceries and in supermarkets. This soup is usually popular in the Spring, when the fava beans are small and tender. One to two tablespoons of barley is sometimes added to the soup. If you choose to do this, use quick cooking barley and add during the last 10 to 15 minutes of simmering.

Pea Soup

Soppa tal-Piżelli

Ingredients

1 large onion, peeled and chopped
2 tablespoons olive or other vegetable oil
1 cup dried split peas
2 large potatoes, peeled and chopped
2 carrots, peeled and chopped
1 stalk celery, chopped
2 to 3 sprigs fresh Italian parsley
2 to 3 sprigs mint
salt and freshly ground pepper
5 cups cold water
5 cups vegetable or chicken stock
1 cup sour cream, yogurt, or milk
sprigs of curly parsley for garnish
loaf of crusty bread

Method

In large stockpot, sauté onion in olive oil until the onion becomes translucent, usually between 5 and 10 minutes. Add split peas, potatoes, carrots, celery, parsley, mint, salt and pepper to taste. Cover with water and stock. Simmer over medium heat until the vegetables are tender, approximately 45 minutes to one hour. Remove from heat. Cool. In blender or food processor, purée the soup on pulse speed until smooth. Transfer to stockpot. Add sour cream. Heat gently for approximately five minutes, stirring to make certain the soup remains smooth. Ladle into soup bowls. Garnish with sprigs of curly parsley.

Serve piping hot with a loaf of crusty bread, salad, and cheeselettes. 6 to 8 servings.

Variations

Many Maltese families will omit the cream, yogurt, or milk; others will use a leftover pork or ham bone. Another choice is adding 1 to 2 slices of bacon to this soup. Some families will add cubed, stale crusty bread that has been deep-fried in olive oil to the soup at the time of serving.

Chick-pea Soup

Soppa taċ-Ċi'ri

Ingredients

2 large onions, peeled and chopped finely
1 to 4 cloves garlic, peeled and minced
2 tablespoons olive or other vegetable oil
1 pound dried chick-peas soaked overnight, or one can (19 ounces) ready-to-use chick-peas, drained and well rinsed
1 stalk celery, chopped
1 to 3 sprigs Italian parsley, minced
1 teaspoon cumin (optional)
salt and freshly ground pepper
9 cups cold water
3 cups vegetable, beef, or chicken stock
sprigs of curly parsley for garnish
loaf of crusty bread

Method

In large stockpot, sauté onion and garlic in olive oil until onion becomes translucent, usually between 5 and 10 minutes. Add chick-peas, celery, parsley, cumin, and salt and pepper to taste. Cover with water and stock. Simmer for approximately 1 hour until the chickpeas are soft. The soup can be served as is, but many people prefer to purée the soup in a food processor or blender to create a smoother texture. Garnish with curly parsley.

Serve with a loaf of crusty bread, cheeselettes, or a salad.

6 to 8 servings.

Kitchen Notes

Some families will add to the soup cubed, stale crusty bread that has been deep fried in olive oil at the time of serving.

Courgette Soup

Soppa tal-Qara' Bagħli

This is yet another simple but quite satisfying soup.

Ingredients

1 to 2 large onions, peeled and chopped
4 tablespoons unsalted butter or margarine, divided
1 to 2 pounds courgette squash, peeled
3 large potatoes, peeled and chopped
1 to 2 stalks celery
salt and freshly ground pepper
6 cups cold water
4 cups vegetable stock
loaf of crusty bread

Method

In a large stockpot, sauté the onions in 2 tablespoons butter until the onion becomes transparent, usually between 5 and 10 minutes. Add squash, potatoes, celery, and salt and pepper to taste. Cover with water and stock. Bring to a boil and then simmer for approximately 45 minutes to an hour until the vegetables are tender. Remove from heat. Cool. In blender or food processor, purée until smooth. Return the soup to the stockpot and add remaining butter. Ladle into soup bowls.

Serve piping hot with a salad and a loaf of crusty bread.

6 to 8 servings.

Variations

Some Maltese families will add a dollop of ricotta and freshly grated Parmesan cheese as a topping for this soup.

Kitchen Notes

These squash are different than most available in North America. A good substitute might be the small, green-yellow round bottom squash found in summer food markets. In Malta, courgettes are dark squash found in summer food markets. In Malta, courgettes are dark green, small, and round. They do not resemble zucchini, although some Maltese families (especially those with home gardens) in North America will use the zucchini or other squash they grow to make this soup.

Jerusalem Artichoke and Potato Soup

Soppa ta' l-Artiċokks u l-Patata

This recipe was provided by Josephine Caruana, a good friend's mother living in Malta.

Ingredients

2 tablespoons unsalted butter or margarine
1 large onion, peeled and chopped
2 cloves garlic, peeled and crushed
3 potatoes, peeled and diced
3 pounds Jerusalem artichokes, cleaned, and chopped
5 cups chicken or vegetable stock
3 cups cold water
salt and white pepper
1 cup cream
2 to 3 sprigs fresh Italian parsley, minced
loaf of crusty bread

Method

In large stockpot, melt unsalted butter over low heat. Add the onion and garlic, and sauté until soft. Add the potatoes and Jerusalem artichokes and sauté for 2 minutes. Cover with stock and water. Add salt and pepper to taste. Cover and simmer until the potatoes and artichokes become soft. Remove from heat and cool. Purée cooled soup in a food processor or blender. Stir in the cream, and sprinkle with parsley just before serving.

Serve with a loaf of crusty bread.

6 to 8 servings.

Spinach Soup

Soppa ta' l-Ispinaci

Ingredients

2 large onions, peeled and chopped
1 to 2 cloves garlic, peeled and chopped
2 tablespoons olive or other vegetable oil
1 pound lean lamb for stew, cut into one-inch cubes
1 to 2 carrots, peeled and sliced
1 teaspoon chopped fresh dill
salt and freshly ground pepper
8 cups cold water
4 cups vegetable stock
1 cup uncooked rice or quick cooking barley
1 pound spinach or chard (rinsed, chopped, and steamed)
loaf of crusty bread

Method

In large stockpot, sauté onions and garlic in olive oil, until the onion becomes translucent, usually between 5 and 10 minutes. Add lamb and continuing sautéing for another 10 minutes. Remove from heat. Drain off and discard excess fat. Add carrots, dill, and salt and pepper to taste. Cover with water and stock. Bring to a boil. Simmer for approximately one hour. Bring to a boil again. Add rice or barley. Reduce heat. Stir frequently, making certain the rice or barley does not clump together. At the conclusion of cooking, add the steamed spinach. Stir. Heat for another 5 minutes.

Serve piping hot with a loaf of crusty bread.

6 to 8 servings.

Kitchen Notes

Some Maltese families prefer using beef shin instead of lamb for this soup.

Like most soups, this one can be refrigerated, then frozen and used at another time. The meat can be served separately. If you choose not to use the soup immediately, refrigerate for several hours and skim off and discard the excess fat.

Pumpkin Soup

Soppa tal-Qara'Aħmar

Ingredients

1 large onion, peeled and chopped
2 tablespoons olive or other vegetable oil
1 large sweet or cheese pumpkin, approximately 1½ pounds, skin removed, scooped out, seeded, and chopped
3 carrots, peeled and sliced
1 stalk celery, chopped
salt and freshly ground pepper
4 cups cold water
3 cups vegetable stock
½ cup cooked pastina or other small pasta (optional)
2 to 3 sprigs Italian parsley, minced
ricotta cheese or 3 to 4 cheeselettes, for topping

Method

In large saucepot, sauté onion in olive oil until it becomes translucent, usually between 5 and 10 minutes. Add pumpkin, carrots, celery, and salt and pepper to taste. Cover with water and stock. Simmer until vegetables are tender. Remove from heat. Cool. Purée soup in blender or food processor. Add cooked pastina and parsley to the soup at the table.

Serve with a dollop of ricotta or fresh *gbejniet,* if available.

4 to 6 servings.

Chestnut and Cocoa Soup

Imbuljuta

Several Maltese friends have fond memories of coming home on a wintery afternoon and having their mother or grandmother prepare this soup for them. One friend noted: "As kids we used to enjoy immensely imbuljuta on those cold winter nights. We didn't have any heat at home in Zejtun. You can imagine how a bowl of steaming imbuljuta was welcome. Thinking about it makes me want to have some now."

Ingredients

1½ pounds fresh chestnuts or 1 pound canned chestnuts
6 cups cold water
2 tablespoons unsweetened cocoa plus 2 tablespoons sugar, or 3 tablespoons sweetened cocoa
zest from one orange or tangerine
½ teaspoon cinnamon (optional)
½ teaspoon cloves (optional)
dash nutmeg (optional)

Method

For fresh chestnuts:

Wash chestnuts thoroughly. With a serrated knife, carefully cut a cross-hatch on the underside of each chestnut and place them in boiling water for approximately 15 minutes. Remove from water. Carefully peel away shells from nut meat. Discard water. Rinse nut meats to make certain they are free from shells. Chop coarsely.

Simmer nut meats in water for approximately 30 to 40 minutes until tender. Add cocoa, zest, cinnamon, cloves, and nutmeg. Simmer another 10 minutes. Ladle in soup bowls or large mugs.

Serve piping hot.

4 to 5 servings.

Variations

Many Maltese families choose to use the zest of a tangerine instead of an orange, especially when tangerines are plentiful in the winter.

Some cooks will add a tablespoon of either rum or red wine to the soup. Others will add a bay leaf during simmering.

As a serving alternative, some Maltese families in North America, such as mine, purée the soup in a food processor or blender and serve it as a hot drink, just as many people might serve hot cocoa.

Meat Broth

Brodu tal-Laħam

This is a very simple soup that freezes well and is often considered the equivalent of "Jewish penicillin" when a family member is ill or just "under the weather."

Ingredients

2 large onions, peeled and chopped
1 to 2 tablespoons olive or other vegetable oil
1 to 2 pounds beef shin
2 large carrots, peeled and sliced
1 to 2 stalks celery, chopped
1 teaspoon tomato paste
salt and freshly ground pepper
10 cups cold water
4 cups beef stock
1 pound fresh spinach, stems removed, finely chopped
½ cup cooked rice or small pasta variety
loaf of crusty bread
ricotta cheese or 3 to 4 cheeselettes (optional)

Method

In large kettle or stockpot, sauté onion in olive oil until the onion becomes translucent, usually between 5 and 10 minutes. Add meat, carrots, celery, tomato paste, and salt and pepper to taste. Cover with water and stock. Bring to a boil and simmer for 45 minutes to one hour, making certain the meat is cooked and the vegetables are tender. Add the chopped spinach during the final 15 minutes of simmering. Remove from heat. Fill individual soup bowls with either the cooked pasta or rice, and ladle soup over it.

Serve piping hot with cheeselettes or a dollop of ricotta cheese, and a loaf of crusty bread.

6 to 8 servings.

Kitchen Notes

To reduce the fat content of this soup, remove from heat and refrigerate for several hours. Skim off and discard hardened fat on the top of soup and reheat to serve.

Kidney Soup

Soppa tal-Kliewi

Ingredients

2 tablespoons unsalted butter or margarine
1 slice lean bacon
1 large onion, peeled and chopped
1 pound beef or lamb kidneys, cleaned, rinsed, and sliced
2 stalks celery, chopped
3 large carrots, peeled and sliced
1 to 2 sprigs Italian parsley, minced
1 to 2 sprigs fresh rosemary
salt and freshly ground pepper
10 cups cold water
2 cups cooked rice

Method

In large stockpot, melt unsalted butter over low heat. Add bacon and onion and sauté until onion is translucent, usually between 5 and 10 minutes. Pour off and discard excess fat. Add kidneys, celery, carrots, parsley, rosemary, and salt and pepper to taste. Cover with water. Simmer for 1½ to 2 hours, until kidneys are tender.

Serve over cooked rice.

6 to 8 servings.

Kitchen Notes

To reduce the fat content of this soup, remove from heat and refrigerate for several hours. Skim off and discard hardened fat on the top of soup and reheat to serve.

Fish and Garlic Soup

Aljotta

This recipe is adapted from Chef Tony Spiteri, Ic-Cima Restaurant, Xlendi Bay, Gozo.

Ingredients

2 large onions, peeled and chopped
8 to 10 cloves garlic, peeled and minced
3 tablespoons olive or vegetable oil
3 potatoes, peeled and sliced
3 large tomatoes, peeled and chopped or 1 can (6 ounces) tomato paste
1 to 2 sprigs fresh basil, torn
1 to 2 sprigs fresh mint, torn
2 to 3 sprigs fresh marjoram
salt and freshly ground pepper
12 cups cold water
1 to 2 pounds fresh, cleaned small fish. Rock fish, which may not be available in North America, typically is used in Malta.
½ cup freshly shelled or frozen peas or ½ cup fresh fava beans, (in season)
gbejniet or other cheeselettes, for topping

Method

In large kettle or stockpot, sauté chopped onion and garlic cloves in olive oil until the onion becomes translucent, usually between 5 to 10 minutes. Add potatoes, tomatoes, basil, mint, marjoram, and salt and pepper to taste. Cover with water and simmer. When the potatoes are almost cooked, place the fish in a strainer or steamer basket and immerse it in the soup for ½ hour. As an alternative, place fish in muslin, tie securely, and place in soup. Add peas or fava beans to soup.

Remove fish from soup and debone. The deboned fish can be eaten separately or put back into the soup.

Ladle the soup into individual bowls.

Serve with *gbejniet* or other cheeselettes.

6 to 8 servings.

Kitchen Notes

This soup is frequently eaten with slices of shelled, hard-boiled egg or Maltese bread, fried in olive oil.

Semolina Soup

Soppa tas-Smid

Ingredients

2 cloves garlic, crushed
2 tablespoons olive or vegetable oil
2 to 3 large, ripe tomatoes, peeled and chopped or 1 can (28 ounces) peeled tomatoes can be substituted
1 to 3 sprigs Italian parsley, minced
1 large bay leaf
6 cups cold water
3 cups vegetable stock
salt and freshly ground pepper
3 tablespoons semolina (not semolina flour)
freshly grated Parmesan cheese, for topping

Method

In large stockpot, sauté garlic in olive oil. Add tomatoes, parsley, and bay leaf. Cover with water and vegetable stock, and salt and pepper to taste. Bring to a boil. Remove from heat and add semolina. Boil for approximately 15 minutes and then simmer for another 15 minutes, making certain the semolina does not become lumpy. Remove bay leaf and discard. Ladle into soup bowls. Sprinkle with grated cheese at the table.

Serve hot.

4 to 6 servings.

Kitchen Notes

More traditional recipes for this soup call for a raw egg to be added in the last few minutes of simmering. A shelled, sliced, hard-boiled egg is often served at the table instead.

Chapter 4

Vegetables

Ħaxix

Meat-stuffed Baked Peppers

Bżar Aħdar Mimli bil-Laħam

Ingredients

4 large bell peppers, tops removed
3 to 4 cups prepared tomato sauce or meat sauce, chilled
2 cups cooked, white rice
2 eggs, well beaten (consider using 1 egg plus one egg white)
4 teaspoons freshly grated Parmesan cheese
salt and freshly ground pepper

Method

Preheat the oven to 350°F.

Core and seed each pepper. Rinse under cold water. Pat dry inside and out with paper towels. Set aside. In a large bowl, mix tomato sauce, cooked white rice, and well beaten eggs. Add two tablespoons of the freshly grated Parmesan cheese, and salt and pepper to taste. Carefully fill each pepper with the rice mixture. Sprinkle remaining Parmesan cheese on top of each pepper. Bake for approximately 35 minutes until the filling becomes crunchy on top.

Serve either hot or cold.

4 servings.

Variations

In the summer, some families will substitute cooked and flaked fish, such as *lampuki* or fresh tuna, instead of the meat.

Kitchen Notes

See Sauce Recipes in Chapter 5. In our home, we make a large quantity of meat sauce for a dish such as *mqarrun fil-forn* and instead of freezing the leftover sauce, use it for either stuffed peppers or stuffed eggplant.

Stuffed Eggplant 1

Brinġiel Mimli 1

Carmen Grech Polise says this was always a favorite in her household.

Ingredients

1 large eggplant
1 large onion, peeled and diced (divided)
2 cloves garlic, peeled and minced
4 tablespoons olive or other vegetable oil
¾ to 1 pound lean ground beef
2 to 3 cups prepared tomato sauce
1 to 2 eggs, well beaten
salt and freshly ground pepper
4 teaspoons freshly grated Parmesan cheese
2 slices bacon (optional)
3 large potatoes, peeled and diced
2 large carrots, peeled and diced
1 tablespoon olive oil (for sprinkling)

Method

Preheat the oven to 350°F.

Wash eggplant and trim off stem. Slice lengthwise. Carefully scoop out flesh and dice evenly. Place eggplant shells and flesh in cold water with salt for approximately 15 minutes. (See Kitchen Notes, p. 103) Set aside. Drain and pat dry eggplant shells and the flesh.

In a large skillet, sauté half of the onion and all of the garlic in olive oil until the onion becomes translucent, usually between 5 and 10 minutes. Add eggplant cubes and ground beef. Cook over low heat until the eggplant becomes soft and the meat is no longer pink. Drain some of the fat from pan (traditional Maltese leave all the oil!). Return to heat and add the tomato sauce, eggs, salt and pepper to taste, and Parmesan cheese. Continue simmering until eggs are cooked and cheese has melted. Remove from heat. Cool.

Place the two drained eggplant halves in a casserole dish. Carefully spoon prepared meat-sauce filling into the eggplant halves and place a slice of bacon on top of each. Surround eggplant with potatoes, carrots, and the remaining onions. Fill dish with water (halfway), drizzle additional oil over potatoes, carrots, and onions, and sprinkle additional salt and pepper. Bake for approximately one hour until the ground beef is crusty on the top of the eggplant. If potatoes remain uncooked after one hour, remove eggplant halves and cover them with foil for another 15 to 20 minutes of baking. During baking, baste eggplant with pan juices, and keep juices from drying out.

Serve either hot or cold.

2 servings.

Kitchen Notes

Eggplant slices should be soaked in cold water and kosher salt for approximately 15 minutes, rinsed, and then patted dried with paper towels to eliminate the bitterness.

Stuffed Eggplant 2

Brinġiel Mimli 2

This is a favorite in the Caruana household.

Ingredients

1 large eggplant
2 to 3 cups prepared tomato sauce with lean ground meat
1 to 2 cups cooked white rice
1 egg, well beaten
2 to 3 tablespoons freshly grated Parmesan cheese

Method

Preheat the oven to 350°F.

Wash and trim off end of eggplant. Carefully scoop out and dice the flesh evenly. Place eggplant shells and flesh in cold water with salt for approximately 15 minutes. (See Kitchen Notes, p. 103) Set aside. Drain and pat dry eggplant shells and flesh.

Add chopped eggplant to meat sauce and heat for approximately 35 minutes. Remove sauce from heat and cool. Add white rice and egg to sauce. Mix well. Carefully pour sauce/rice mixture into eggplant shells. Top with Parmesan cheese. Bake in a well-greased or oiled casserole dish for approximately 35 to 45 minutes, until the rice/meat mixture becomes crunchy.

Serve either hot or cold.

2 servings.

Fried Eggplant

Bringiel Moqli

Ingredients

all-purpose, unbleached flour for dredging
salt and and freshly ground pepper
2 large eggplants, stems removed, sliced (See Kitchen Notes, p. 103)
olive or other oil suitable for frying

Method

Season flour with salt and pepper. In large flat-bottomed dish, dredge eggplant slices in seasoned flour. Set aside. Heat olive oil in skillet. Fry individual slices of eggplant, turning over frequently until each side is crisp. Drain on absorbent paper.

Serve hot.

4 to 6 servings.

Variations

Many Maltese cooks choose to use bread crumbs instead of the flour. To make it this way, first dip each eggplant slice in 2 well-beaten eggs or 1 egg plus one egg white. Then, coat with bread crumbs that have been seasoned with salt and freshly ground pepper before frying.

Eggplant Appetizer

Bringiel Agrodolce

Although this dish is often part of a platter of appetizers before a meal, many Maltese families serve it as a vegetable side dish. However you serve this dish, you'll find it's a delicious way to use the eggplants that are growing in your summer garden or available at local fruit stands.

Ingredients

1 to 2 large onions, peeled and diced
2 to 3 cloves garlic, peeled and minced
2 tablespoons olive or other vegetable oil
2 large eggplants, peeled, diced, and soaked in salt water for 15 minutes and then rinsed
3 large ripe tomatoes, chopped
1 to 2 sprigs fresh mint, minced
salt and freshly ground pepper
1 to 2 cups cold water or vegetable stock
1 teaspoon sugar
3 teaspoons red wine vinegar

Method

In a large skillet, sauté onion and garlic in olive oil until onion becomes translucent, usually between 5 and 10 minutes. Add eggplant, tomatoes, mint, and salt and pepper to taste. Add enough water or stock to cover vegetables. Simmer until eggplant is tender, approximately 35 minutes. Remove from heat. Add sugar and vinegar. Mix thoroughly and refrigerate.

Serve cold.

3 to 4 servings.

Meat-stuffed Marrows (Squash)

Qara' Bagħli Mimli bil-Laħam

Ingredients

2 tablespoons olive or other vegetable oil

1 to 2 cups unseasoned bread crumbs moistened, or 1 to 2 cups cooked long-grain white rice

2 to 3 cloves garlic, peeled and minced

3 to 4 sprigs Italian parsley, minced

2 to 3 sprigs marjoram, minced

salt and freshly ground pepper

1 cup freshly prepared tomato sauce with meat

1 egg, well beaten

4 courgette squash, tops removed, inside carefully scooped out. (Zucchini or other squash may be substituted.)

3 to 4 tablespoons freshly grated Parmesan cheese

Method

Preheat the oven to 350°F.

Drizzle olive or other vegetable oil on bottom of casserole dish. Set aside.

In large bowl, mix bread crumbs or rice with garlic, parsley, marjoram, and salt and pepper to taste. Add tomato sauce and egg. Mix well.

Carefully spoon sauce mixture into individual squashes. Top with Parmesan cheese. Place in casserole dish and bake for approximately 35 minutes, until the top becomes brown.

Serve either hot or cold.

3 to 4 servings.

Ricotta-stuffed Marrows (Squash)

Qara' Bagħli Mimli bl-Irkotta

Ingredients

2 tablespoons olive or other vegetable oil
4 courgette squash, tops removed, inside carefully scooped out (zucchini or other squash may be substituted.)
1 to 2 cups unseasoned bread crumbs, moistened or 1 to 2 cups cooked long-grain white rice
2 to 3 cloves garlic, peeled and crushed
3 to 4 sprigs Italian parsley, minced
2 to 3 sprigs marjoram, minced
salt and freshly ground pepper
1 to 2 cups part-skim or whole-milk ricotta cheese
2 eggs, well-beaten (consider using 1 egg plus 1 egg white)
3 to 4 tablespoons freshly grated, Parmesan cheese

Method

Preheat the oven to 350°F.

Drizzle olive or other vegetable oil on bottom of casserole dish. Set aside.

In large bowl, mix bread crumbs or rice with garlic, parsley, marjoram, and salt and pepper to taste. Add ricotta and egg. Mix well.

Carefully spoon ricotta mixture in individual squashes. Top with Parmesan cheese. Place in casserole dish and bake for approximately 35 minutes, until the top becomes brown.

Serve either hot or cold.

3 to 4 servings.

Cauliflower Fritters

Fritturi tal-Pastard

This is a simple yet satisfying vegetable dish that we often made when we had leftover, cooked cauliflower. It even made my brother a lover of cauliflower.

Ingredients

1 large cauliflower, large stems removed, chopped, and cooked
2 large eggs, well beaten
salt and freshly ground black pepper
olive or other vegetable oil suitable for frying

Method

In a large bowl, mix cooked, chopped cauliflower with beaten eggs. Add salt and pepper to taste. Divide mixture into four portions. Heat oil in heavy skillet and gently drop cauliflower mixture in the skillet. When the cauliflower fritter is cooked on the bottom, turn over with a spatula and continue pan frying until the other side is golden. Place on paper towels to absorb excess oil. Repeat for each portion.

Serve piping hot.

3 to 4 servings.

Cauliflower Stew

Stuffat tal-Pastard

Ingredients

1 large onion, peeled and chopped
2 cloves garlic, peeled and minced
olive or other vegetable oil
2 tablespoons tomato paste
1 large cauliflower, stems removed, broken into florets
1/3 cup golden raisins (sultanas)
10 to 12 green or black pitted olives, sliced
3 cups vegetable stock
1 to 2 cups cold water
salt and freshly ground pepper

Method

In a large skillet, sauté onion and garlic in olive oil until the onion becomes translucent, usually between 5 and 10 minutes. Add tomato paste. Add stock, cauliflower, raisins, and olives. Cover with water. Add salt and pepper to taste. Simmer until cauliflower is tender, approximately 20 to 25 minutes. Add more water if the stew appears to be drying out.

Serve hot.

3 to 4 servings.

Spinach Omelette

Froġa ta' l-Ispinaċi

This is an easy-to-prepare dish and a good way to use left-over spinach.

Ingredients

1 to 2 pounds fresh spinach, well-rinsed, stems removed, steamed, drained, and chopped
2 eggs, well beaten (consider using 1 egg plus 1 egg white)
juice from ½ fresh lemon or 1 tablespoon lemon juice
1 teaspoon fresh dill, minced (optional)
dash nutmeg (optional)
salt and freshly ground pepper
olive or other vegetable oil suitable for pan frying

Method

In a large bowl, mix chopped spinach, eggs, lemon juice, dill, nutmeg, and salt and pepper to taste. Set aside. Heat olive oil in small skillet. Carefully pour one-quarter of the spinach mixture in skillet. Pan fry until bottom becomes brown and crunchy. Turn over with a spatula. Cook until crisp. Place on paper towels to absorb excess oil. Repeat the procedure.

Serve piping hot.

3 to 4 servings.

Variations

Some families like to add a tablespoon or more of Parmesan cheese to the spinach mixture before cooking. Although feta cheese is not typically Maltese, many Maltese families living in Greek neighborhoods such as Astoria, New York, like to add crumbled feta cheese to the spinach mixture before pan frying.

Spinach Pie

Torta ta' l-Ispinaċi

Ingredients

For the pastry:

pastry for a 9-inch double crust pie, see page 273
egg wash

For the filling:

1 large onion, peeled and diced
1 to 2 cloves garlic, peeled and minced
2 tablespoons olive or other vegetable oil
1 pound spinach, well-rinsed, stems removed, steamed, drained, and chopped
10 pitted green olives, chopped
1 can (2 ounces) anchovy filets, drained, well-rinsed, and chopped
1 sprig fresh dill, chopped (optional)
salt and freshly ground pepper
1 cup freshly shelled or frozen peas (optional)
juice from ½ of a fresh lemon or 1 tablespoon lemon juice
1 egg, well-beaten
2 tablespoons freshly grated Parmesan cheese

Method

Preheat the oven to 350°F.

Place a freshly rolled out pie crust on a well-floured pie plate. With a fork, pierce the crust in several places. Pre-bake bottom pie crust for approximately 10 minutes. Ceramic or metal weights can be placed over wax or parchment paper to prevent pie crust from bubbling. Remove from oven and cool. Set aside.

In a large skillet, sauté onion and garlic in olive oil until the onion becomes translucent, usually between 5 and 10 minutes. Add spinach and olives. Stir in chopped anchovies, dill, and salt and pepper to taste. Mix well and heat over low heat. Add peas and lemon juice. Remove from heat. Mix the egg and grated freshly grated Parmesan cheese in a separate bowl. Add egg mixture to spinach mixture. Set aside. Carefully spoon filling in the pre-baked pastry. Cover filling with top pastry. Seal and flute edges. Brush top crust with egg wash. Create vent holes in top crust. Bake for approximately 45 minutes or until crust becomes golden brown.

Serve either hot or cold.

4 to 6 servings.

Fried Pumpkin

Qara' Aħmar Mgħolli

Ingredients

1 large pumpkin, scooped out, seeded, and thinly sliced
all-purpose, unbleached flour for dredging (seasoned with 1 teaspoon mixed spice and ½ teaspoon salt)
vegetable oil sufficient for pan frying

Method

Dredge pumpkin slices in seasoned flour. Set aside. Heat oil in frying pan. Fry pumpkin, turning over frequently until each side is crisp. Drain on absorbent paper.

Serve hot.

3 to 4 servings.

Variations

Many Maltese cooks choose to use bread crumbs instead of the flour. To make it this way, first dip each pumpkin slice in well-beaten egg plus one egg white. Then, coat with bread crumbs that have been seasoned with salt, freshly ground pepper, and mixed spice.

Kitchen Notes

Pumpkin spice, usually a combination of cinnamon, ginger, mace, and cardamon, can be used instead of mixed spice.

Broad Beans with Garlic and Parsley

Ful bit-Tewm u t-Tursin

Ingredients

2 pounds dried fava beans that have been soaked for 48 hours with baking soda and stripped of their two shells; or 2 cans (10 ounces each) fava beans, well-rinsed and drained. (See Kitchen Notes on fava beans, p. 46)
1 quart water
2 to 3 cloves garlic, peeled and minced
5 to 6 tablespoons olive oil
3 to 4 tablespoons red wine vinegar
1 medium onion or shallot, peeled and minced
2 sprigs Italian parsley, minced
2 sprigs mint, minced
salt and freshly ground pepper

Method

In large saucepot, simmer prepared fava beans in water until tender. Drain thoroughly. Season with remaining ingredients. Toss well.

Serve either hot or cold.

3 to 4 servings.

Beans with Garlic

Fażola bit-Tewm

This simple but tasty recipe is a favorite in the Sandro Grima household.

Ingredients

1 can (16 ounces) canoli or butter beans
1 quart cold water
4 to 5 tablespoons olive or other vegetable oil
2 to 3 tablespoons red wine vinegar
1 to 2 sprigs Italian parsley, minced
1 to 2 cloves garlic, peeled and minced
salt and freshly ground pepper

Method

In large saucepot, simmer beans in water until tender. Drain thoroughly. Cool. When beans are at room temperature, add oil, vinegar, parsley, garlic, and salt and pepper. The beans should be left untouched for at least 1 hour before serving.

Serve as part of an appetizer platter or with *hobz biz-zejt.*

3 to 4 servings.

Boiled Jerusalem Artichokes

Artiċokks Mgħolli

Jerusalem artichokes are an often overlooked vegetable in North America although they were discovered on the continent and then imported to Europe. After they are boiled, they can be eaten either hot or cold, salad style.

Ingredients

2 to 3 pounds Jerusalem artichokes (sometimes called sunchokes in North America) cleaned, peeled, and sliced
2 to 3 cloves garlic, peeled and minced
1 to 2 shallots, peeled and minced
3 to 4 sprigs Italian parsley, minced
4 to 5 tablespoons olive oil
2 to 3 tablespoons wine vinegar
salt and freshly ground pepper to taste

Method

Place Jerusalem artichokes in a kettle of boiling water. Cook until tender, approximately 15 minutes. Remove from heat. Drain. Cool.

In medium size bowl, toss garlic, shallots, and parsley in olive oil and vinegar. Add salt and pepper to taste. Drizzle dressing over Jerusalem artichokes.

Serve as a vegetable dish, salad, or as part of an appetizer platter.

3 to 4 servings.

Artichoke Hearts with Pork and Chicken Liver Casserole

Stuffat tal-Qlub tal-Qaqoċċ bil-Fegatini u l-Majjal

Ingredients

1 large onion, peeled and chopped
1 to 2 cloves garlic, peeled and minced
2 tablespoons olive or other vegetable oil
¼ pound chopped pork (chopped beef or sausage removed from its casing may be substituted)
½ pound chicken livers, well rinsed and patted dry
3 to 4 large, ripe tomatoes, peeled and chopped or 1 can (28 ounces) peeled tomatoes or purée
6 artichoke hearts (canned artichoke hearts, well-rinsed and drained can be substituted)
salt and freshly ground pepper
2 sprigs curly parsley for garnish

Method

In a large skillet, sauté onion and garlic in olive oil until the onion becomes translucent, usually between 5 and 10 minutes. Add chopped pork and chicken livers. Cook until the meat is pink. Remove from heat. Drain off and discard excess fat. Add tomatoes, artichoke hearts, and salt and pepper, to taste. Simmer until vegetables are soft. Garnish with curly parsley.

Serve either hot or cold.

3 to 4 servings.

Kitchen Notes

Many Maltese cooks make this dish without the chicken livers.

Artichoke Fritters

Fritturi tal-Qaqoċċ

Ingredients

6 artichoke hearts, chopped (canned artichokes, drained and well-rinsed can be substituted for fresh artichoke hearts)
2 eggs, well beaten (consider using 1 egg plus 1 egg white)
1 to 2 sprigs Italian parsley, minced
salt and freshly ground pepper
olive or other vegetable oil suitable for frying

Method

In a large bowl, mix chopped artichoke hearts, eggs, parsley, and salt and pepper to taste. Divide mixture into four portions. Heat oil in a small, heavy skillet, and gently drop artichoke mixture into the skillet. When the artichoke fritter is cooked on the bottom, turn over with a spatula and continue pan frying until the other side is golden. Drain on paper towels to absorb excess oil. Repeat for each portion.

Serve hot.

3 to 4 servings.

Artichoke Stew with Beans and Peas

Stuffat tal-Qaqoċċ bil-Ful u l-Piżelli

Ingredients

1 large onion, peeled and chopped
1 to 2 cloves cloves garlic, peeled and minced
2 to 3 large ripe tomatoes, peeled and sliced or one can (48 ounces) peeled tomatoes can be substituted
2 tablespoons olive or other vegetable oil
1 to 2 cups cold water or chicken or vegetable stock
2 sprigs Italian parsley, minced
salt and freshly ground pepper
6 to 8 artichoke hearts (canned artichoke hearts that have been rinsed thoroughly and drained can be substituted)
1 cup fava beans (optional)
1 cup freshly shelled or frozen peas

Method

In a large skillet, sauté onions garlic, and tomatoes in olive oil until the tomatoes are tender, approximately 10 to 15 minutes. Cover with stock and add parsley, and salt and pepper to taste. Simmer for 15 minutes. Add artichoke hearts, beans, and peas. Simmer until all vegetables are tender. If mixture appears to be drying out, add water.

Serve hot.

3 to 4 servings.

Kitchen Notes

Many Maltese families prefer using either the peas or fava beans in this dish. If you choose to use dried fava beans either alone or with the peas, make certain they have been soaked for at least 24 hours and peeled. Tender fresh favas, however, usually are preferred for this dish.

Stuffed Artichokes

Qaqoċċ Mimli

Ingredients

4 large artichokes, thoroughly washed, prickly ends clipped, and patted dry
juice from ½ fresh lemon or 1 teaspoon lemon juice

For the filling:

2 cups unseasoned bread crumbs
4 to 6 tablespoons unsalted butter or margarine
1 to 2 large shallots, peeled and minced
1 to 2 cloves garlic, peeled and minced
6 to 8 olives, drained, well rinsed, chopped
1 large tomato, finely chopped
1 hard-boiled egg, shelled and chopped finely
2 tablespoons capers, drained and well rinsed
2 to 3 anchovy fillets drained, well-rinsed, and chopped or 2 ounces ham, shredded and chopped (optional)
1 to 2 sprigs thyme, chopped
salt and freshly ground pepper
vinaigrette dressing or melted butter

Method

Soak the artichokes in a bowl of cold water with lemon juice for for 10 to 15 minutes. Soaking makes them easier to stuff, and the lemon juice helps them retain their color. Drain well and set aside.

In a large bowl, combine bread crumbs and butter, making a coarse meal. Add shallots, garlic, olives, tomatoes, chopped egg, capers, chopped anchovies, thyme, and salt and pepper to taste. Mix well.

Spread apart leaves of each artichoke, starting at the center and moving outward. Using a small spoon, stuff each leaf with the bread crumb mixture. Tie each artichoke securely with kitchen twine. Using tongs, carefully place in pot half full with boiling water, keeping the artichokes as close together as possible. Artichokes should not be totally submerged. Cover. Cook for approximately 45 minutes, or until leaves appear easy to remove. Remove from pot with tongs. Loosen kitchen twine.

Serve with vinaigrette dressing, melted butter, or as is.

4 servings.

Variations

Many Maltese cooks will stuff the artichokes with approximately ½ pound of chopped meat—beef, pork, or a combination of beef and pork—instead of, or in addition to a lesser amount of bread crumbs.

Kitchen Notes

Stuffed artichokes freeze well. Prepare as above, wrap in aluminum foil, and freeze uncooked. To cook the stuffed frozen artichokes, place the still-wrapped artichokes in a covered pot of boiling water for 45 minutes to 1 hour.

Pumpkin and Pork Pie

Torta tal-Qara' Aħmar u l-Majjal

Ingredients

For the pastry:

pastry for a 9-inch double crust pie, recipe pg. 273
egg wash

For the filling:

1 large onion, peeled and chopped
2 tablespoons olive or other vegetable oil
1 pound chopped pork or sausage meat, casing removed
1 large pumpkin, skinned, scooped out, seeded, and chopped
1 to 2 leaves fresh sage, crushed
1 to 2 sprigs fresh thyme, chopped
½ teaspoon mixed spice or ½ teaspoon pumpkin spice (optional)
salt and freshly ground pepper
4 cups cooked, long-grain rice
1 egg, well-beaten

Method

Preheat the oven to 350°F.

Place a freshly rolled out pie crust on a well-floured pie plate. With a fork, pierce the crust in several places. Pre-bake bottom pie crust for approximately 10 minutes. Ceramic or metal weights can be placed over wax or parchment paper to prevent pie crust from bubbling. Remove from oven and cool. Set aside.

In a large skillet, sauté onion in olive oil until the onion becomes translucent, usually between 5 and 10 minutes. Add chopped pork and sauté for approximately 15 minutes. Drain off and discard excess fat. Add pumpkin, sage, thyme, mixed spice, and salt and pepper to taste. Sauté mixture until tender. Remove from heat. Fold in rice and egg, and allow the mixture to cool.

Carefully spoon pumpkin, rice, and pork mixture into a pastry-lined plate. Cover with top crust. Seal and flute edges. Brush top crust with egg wash. Create vent holes in top crust. Bake for approximately 45 minutes or until crust becomes golden brown.

Serve hot.
3 to 4 servings.

Kitchen Notes

Canned, solid pumpkin, not canned pumpkin mix, can be substituted for fresh pumpkin. Reduce cooking time if canned pumpkin is used.

Baked Pumpkin, Rice, and Ricotta Pie

Torta tal-Qara' Aħmar, Ross, u l'Irkotta

Although this is often referred to as pie, it's best described as a casserole.

Ingredients

For the pastry:

pastry for a 9-inch double crust pie, see page 273
egg wash

For the filling:

1 medium pumpkin, skinned, scooped out and chopped
1 to 2 tablespoons unsalted butter or margarine
1 cup cooked long-grain white rice
1 cup whole-milk or part-skim ricotta
½ teaspoon cinnamon
½ teaspoon nutmeg
dash cloves
salt and freshly ground pepper
1 to 2 eggs, well beaten (consider using 1 egg and plus 1 egg white)
2 tablespoons freshly grated Parmesan cheese

Method

Preheat the oven to 350°F.

Place a freshly rolled out pie crust on a well-floured pie plate. With a fork, pierce the crust in several places. Pre-bake bottom pie crust for approximately 10 minutes. Ceramic or metal weights can be placed over wax or parchment paper to prevent pie crust from bubbling. Remove from oven and cool. Set aside.

In a large skillet, sauté the pumpkin in butter until soft. Remove from heat. In a large bowl, combine rice, ricotta, cinnamon, nutmeg, cloves, and salt and pepper to taste. Add pumpkin, egg, and Parmesan cheese. Mix well. Carefully spoon filling in pastry-lined plate. Cover filling with top pastry. Seal and flute edges. Brush top crust with egg wash. Create vent holes in top crust. Bake for approximately 45 minutes or until crust is golden brown.

Serve either hot or cold.

3 to 4 servings.

Kitchen Notes

Canned solid pumpkin, not canned pumpkin mix, can be substituted for fresh pumpkin. Reduce cooking time if canned solid pumpkin is used. Mixed spice can be substituted for the cinnamon, nutmeg, and cloves.

Cabbage with Bacon

Kaboċċi bil-Bejken

Ingredients

3 tablespoons unsalted butter or margarine
1 large cabbage, shredded, boiled, and drained thoroughly
3 to 5 slices lean bacon, cut into small pieces

Method

Heat unsalted butter or margarine in small skillet. Add boiled cabbage and bacon. Cook until bacon is crisp, approximately 15 to 25 minutes. Drain off and discard excess fat.

Serve hot.

3 to 4 servings.

Fried Cabbage with Eggs

Kaboċċi Mimlija bil-Bajd

Ingredients

1 large cabbage, boiled, drained, and shredded
2 eggs, well beaten (consider using 1 egg plus 1 egg white)
½ teaspoon cumin (optional)
1 to 2 sprigs parsley, minced
salt and freshly ground pepper
2 tablespoons unsalted butter or margarine

Method

In a large bowl, mix cabbage, eggs, cumin, parsley, and salt and pepper to taste. Set aside. Heat butter or margarine in small skillet. Pour a portion of the mixture in the skillet. Cook until eggs have set. Remove and drain on absorbent paper. Repeat with other portions.

Serve hot.

3 to 4 servings.

Stuffed Cabbage Leaves with Meat

Kaboċċi Mimlijin bil-Laħam

Ingredients

1 large cabbage, leaves removed, washed, and patted dry
4 to 6 cups boiling water
1 large onion, peeled and sliced
1 to 2 cloves garlic, peeled and minced
2 tablespoons olive oil
¾ pound lean ground beef or pork, or a combination
2 tablespoons tomato paste
salt and freshly ground pepper to taste
1 egg, well-beaten
4 teaspoons freshly grated Parmesan cheese

Method

In large bowl, pour boiling water over separated cabbage leaves. Set aside for 15 to 20 minutes.

In a large skillet, sauté onion and garlic in olive oil until the onion becomes translucent, usually between 5 and 10 minutes. Add meat, tomato paste, and salt and pepper to taste. Cook until the meat turns pink. Remove from heat. Drain off and discard excess fat. Cool.

Add egg and Parmesan cheese to meat mixture. Carefully spoon meat mixture onto individual cabbage leaves. Roll up and tie with kitchen twine. Carefully place leaves in skillet with a small amount of water. Simmer for approximately 30 to 45 minutes or until the cabbage leaves are tender. Remove twine.

Serve immediately.

3 to 4 servings.

Kohlrabi Fritters

Fritturi tal-Ġidra

Although kohlrabi is often associated with Eastern European cooking, it is a staple in many Maltese homes. As a child living outside of New York City I saw gidra proudly growing in the gardens of many Maltese American friends and families, including my Uncle Philip's. Often, my family would eat peeled and thinly sliced gidra raw; other families added gidra to soup. In many other homes, gidra would be fried, similar to the recipe below.

Ingredients

3 large kohlrabi, washed, peeled, and thinly sliced, matchstick style
flour for dredging, seasoned with salt and white pepper
2 eggs well beaten (consider using 1 egg, plus 1 egg white)
olive or other oil suitable for frying

Method

In flat-bottomed plate, dredge the kohlrabi in seasoned flour. In another bowl, dip each floured slice in the beaten egg. Set aside.

Heat oil in a large skillet. Carefully fry kohlrabi slices, turning over to make certain both sides are crisp. Remove from heat. Drain on absorbent paper.

Serve hot.

3 to 4 servings.

Roasted Potatoes

Patata l-Forn

Ingredients

4 large potatoes, peeled and sliced thinly
1 large onion, peeled and sliced
1 clove garlic, crushed (optional)
2 sprigs Italian parsley, minced
1 teaspoon crushed dried rosemary or stripped off leaves of 1 to 2 pieces of fresh rosemary
salt and freshly ground pepper
4 tablespoons olive or other vegetable oil
water

Method

Preheat the oven to 350°F.

On the bottom of a well-greased pie plate or ceramic casserole dish, neatly arrange potato slices. Carefully place onions and garlic on top of the potatoes. Season with parsley, rosemary, and salt and pepper to taste. Drizzle olive oil and water on top. Turn over onions and potatoes at least once during baking. Bake for approximately 45 minutes, until potatoes and onions are soft.

Serve hot.

3 to 4 servings.

Potatoes with Oil and Parsley

Patata bit-Tursin u Żejt

This is another one of those simple, yet very satisfying dishes I remember from my childhood and prepare today when I am in a hurry. Some people might call this a vegetable dish, although many people might look at it as a salad, especially if you choose to make it with shelled hard-boiled eggs and olives as do several Maltese friends.

Ingredients

4 to 5 large potatoes, peeled, boiled, sliced, and chilled
3 to 4 large sprigs Italian parsley, chopped
salt and freshly ground pepper
¼ cup olive oil
3 to 4 hard-boiled eggs, shelled and sliced (optional)
4 to 5 tablespoons sliced black olives, (optional)

Method

In a large bowl, carefully toss sliced potatoes with chopped parsley and salt and pepper to taste. Drizzle the olive oil over the potatoes. If using eggs and olives, add at this time and mix gently. Chill until ready to serve.

Serve cold.

3 to 4 servings.

Chapter 5

Sauces

Zlazi

Caper Sauce

Zalza tal-Kappar

Ingredients

1 large onion, peeled and chopped
1 to 2 cloves garlic, crushed
2 tablespoons olive or other vegetable oil
3 to 4 large ripe tomatoes, peeled and chopped or 1 can (28 ounces) peeled or crushed tomatoes
2 tablespoons tomato paste
1 cup vegetable or chicken stock
1 cup cold water
2 to 3 tablespoons capers, drained and well-rinsed
10 green olives, pitted and chopped
1 to 2 sprigs Italian parsley, minced
1 to 2 sprigs fresh mint, minced
salt and freshly ground pepper

Method

In large saucepot, sauté onion and garlic in olive oil until onion becomes translucent, usually between 5 and 10 minutes. Add tomatoes and tomato paste. Cover with stock and water. Bring to a boil and then simmer for approximately 15 minutes until the sauce begins to thicken. Add capers, olives, parsley, mint, and salt and pepper to taste. Simmer for another 15 to 25 minutes. Add more water if sauce appears to be drying out.

Serve with spaghetti, pasta, fish, or steak.

Makes approximately 2 cups of sauce.

Tomato Sauce

Zalza tat-Tadam

Although many recipes call for tomato sauce, and canned or bottled tomato sauce may be used, you might want to make your own from scratch. If you have fresh tomatoes from the garden, green grocer, or choose to use canned tomatoes, try this. This sauce, like most, freezes well and can be thawed and heated for use at a later time.

Ingredients

2 large shallots, peeled and minced or 1 large onion, peeled and chopped finely
1 to 3 cloves garlic, peeled and minced
2 tablespoons olive or other vegetable oil
3 to 4 large, ripe tomatoes, peeled, or 1 can (28 ounces) peeled or crushed tomatoes
1 large frying pepper, seeded and chopped
1 cup cold water
2 cups vegetable stock
1 sprig mint
1 rib fresh celery
½ teaspoon fresh oregano
1 bay leaf
1 to 2 sprigs Italian parsley, minced
salt and freshly ground pepper

Method

In large saucepot, sauté shallots and garlic in olive oil until the shallots become translucent, usually between 5 and 10 minutes. Add tomatoes and frying pepper and sauté for another 5 to 10 minutes. Cover with water and stock. Add mint, celery, oregano, bay leaf, parsley, and salt and pepper to taste. Simmer for approximately 45 minutes to 1 hour until the sauce begins to thicken. Add more water if sauce appears to be drying out. Remove bay leaf and celery rib before serving.

Serve with spaghetti, pasta, fish, or meat.

Makes approximately 2 to 3 cups sauce.

Tomato Sauce with Corned Beef

Zalza bil-Bulibif

This is a very simple and quick sauce that often serves as the filling for the very popular pastizzi tal-pizelli.

Ingredients

1 large onion, peeled and minced
1 to 2 cloves garlic, peeled and minced
2 tablespoons olive or other vegetable oil
2 cans (15 ounces each) tomato sauce
1 can (12 ounces) corned beef, excess fat scraped off, then flaked
1 to 2 leaves fresh basil or 1 teaspoon dried basil leaves, crushed
2 to 3 sprigs Italian parsley, minced
salt and freshly ground pepper
2 cup cold water or beef stock
1 cup freshly shelled or frozen peas (split peas that have been soaked for 15 minutes prior to cooking can be substituted)

Method

In a large skillet, sauté onion and garlic in olive oil until the onion becomes translucent, usually between 5 and 10 minutes. Add tomato sauce, corned beef, basil, parsley, and salt and pepper to taste. Cover with water or stock. Simmer for another 15 to 20 minutes. Mix well and then add the peas. Simmer for another 5 to 10 minutes, until the peas are very tender. Add more water if sauce appears to be drying out.

Serve with pasta or spaghetti.

Makes 2 to 3 cups sauce.

Tomato Sauce with Ham

Zalza bil-Perżut

Ingredients

1 large onion, peeled and minced
1 to 2 cloves garlic, peeled and minced
2 tablespoons olive or other vegetable oil
2 cans (15 ounces each) tomato sauce
1 large ham bone (usually leftover from a pork roast)
3 large sprigs Italian parsley, minced
salt and freshly ground pepper
2 cups cold water or beef stock
1 cup freshly shelled or frozen peas (split peas that have been soaked for 15 minutes prior to cooking can be substituted)

Method

In a large skillet, sauté onion and garlic in olive until the onion becomes translucent, usually between 5 and 10 minutes. Add tomato sauce, ham bone, parsley, and salt and pepper to taste. Cover with water or stock. Simmer for another 10 to 20 minutes. Mix well, and then add the peas. Simmer for another 5 to 10 minutes, until the peas are very tender. Add more water if sauce appears to be drying out. Remove from heat.

Serve with pasta or spaghetti.

Makes 2 to 3 cups sauce.

Tomato Sauce with Bacon

Zalza bil-Bejken

Ingredients

1 large onion, peeled and minced
1 to 2 cloves garlic, peeled and minced
2 tablespoons olive or other vegetable oil
3 to 4 slices bacon
2 cans (15 ounces each) tomato sauce
3 large sprigs Italian parsley, minced
salt and freshly ground pepper
2 cups cold water or vegetable or beef stock
1 cup freshly shelled or frozen peas (split peas that have been soaked for 15 minutes prior to cooking can be substituted)

Method

In a large skillet, sauté onions and garlic in olive oil until the onion becomes translucent, usually between 5 and 10 minutes. Add bacon and saute for another 5 minutes. Drain off and discard excess fat. Add tomato sauce, parsley, and salt and pepper to taste. Cover with water or stock. Simmer for another 15 to 20 minutes. Mix well and then add the peas. Simmer for another 5 to 10 minutes, until the peas are very tender. Add more water if the sauce appears to be drying out. Remove from heat.

Serve with pasta or spaghetti.

Makes 2 to 3 cups sauce.

Eggplant Sauce

Zalza tal-Brinġiel

Ingredients

1 large onion, peeled and diced
1 to 2 cloves garlic, peeled and minced
2 tablespoons olive or other vegetable oil
1 large eggplant, peeled and diced, soaked in kosher salt for 15 minutes, rinsed and patted dry
3 to 4 large ripe tomatoes, chopped or 1 can (28 ounces) peeled or crushed tomatoes
1 to 2 sprigs Italian parsley, minced
1 rib celery
1 bay leaf
2 to 3 fresh basil leaves torn or 1 teaspoon basil, crushed
salt and freshly ground pepper
3 cups cold water, vegetable, or beef stock (or a combination of water and stock)

Method

In large saucepot, sauté onion, and garlic in olive oil until onion becomes translucent, usually between 5 and 10 minutes. Add eggplant, tomatoes, parsley, celery, bay leaf, basil, and salt and pepper to taste. Cover with water and stock. Bring to a boil and then simmer for approximately 30 minutes until sauce begins to thicken. Add more water if sauce appears to be drying out. Remove celery and bay leaf before serving.

Serve with spaghetti, pasta, fish, or meat.

Makes 2 to 3 cups sauce.

Variations

Some families use eggplant sauce as a filling for a torta or pie. In this case, make certain the eggplant is not overcooked. Eggplant sauce can be mixed with cooked pasta and served with ricotta and Parmesan cheese for a very satisfying meal. It also can be a side dish, served with a loaf of crusty bread, cheese and a salad.

Piquant Sauce

Zalza Pikkanti

This sauce is always a favorite for fish and can be used for pasta as well.

Ingredients

1 large onion, peeled and minced
2 tablespoons olive or other vegetable oil
2 tablespoons tomato paste
1 tablespoon red wine vinegar
1 teaspoon granulated sugar
5 to 8 green olives, drained, well-rinsed, and chopped
2 tablespoons capers, drained, well-rinsed, and chopped
salt and freshly ground pepper
3 cups cold water

Method

In a large skillet, sauté the onion in olive oil until the onion becomes translucent, usually between 5 and 10 minutes. Add tomato paste, vinegar, sugar, olives, capers, and salt and pepper to taste. Cover with water. Simmer for approximately 45 minutes until the sauce begins to thicken. Add more water if sauce appears to be drying out.

Serve cold over fish or meat.

Makes 2 to 3 cups sauce.

Variations

Sometimes vegetable stock is substituted for the water.

Octopus Sauce

Zalza tal-Qarnita

Ingredients

1 large onion, peeled and chopped
1 to 2 cloves garlic, peeled and minced
2 tablespoons olive or other vegetable oil
Approximately 2 pounds cleaned, fresh octopus, sliced into small pieces or frozen octopus, thawed and chopped
3 large ripe tomatoes, chopped or 1 can (28 ounces) peeled tomatoes or crushed tomatoes
2 tablespoons tomato paste
1 to 3 sprigs Italian parsley, minced
1 sprig fresh mint, minced
1 bay leaf
5 cups cold water
3 cups fish stock
salt and freshly ground pepper

Method

In a large skillet, sauté onion and garlic in olive oil until onion becomes translucent, usually between 5 and 10 minutes. Add octopus, tomatoes, tomato paste, parsley, mint, bay leaf, and salt and pepper to taste. Cover with water and stock. Simmer until the octopus is tender, approximately 90 minutes. Add more water if sauce appears to be drying out. Remove bay leaf before serving.

Serve with pasta, spaghetti, or rice. Makes 2 to 3 cups sauce.

Calamari Sauce

Zalza tal-Klamari

Follow the recipe above except to substitute 2 pounds of cleaned (ink bags removed) squid, fresh or thawed, cut into pieces instead of the octopus.

Anchovy Sauce

Zalza ta' l-Inċova

Ingredients

1 large onion, peeled and minced
2 to 3 cloves garlic, minced
2 tablespoons olive or other vegetable oil
3 to 4 large, ripe tomatoes, peeled, seeded, and chopped or 1 can (28 ounces) peeled or crushed tomatoes
2 tablespoons tomato paste
1 can (2 ounces) or jar (3½ ounces) anchovy fillets, drained, well-rinsed, and chopped
1 bay leaf
salt and freshly ground pepper
2 cups fish stock
1 cup cold water

Method

In a large skillet, sauté onion and garlic in olive oil until the onion becomes translucent, usually between 5 and 10 minutes. Add tomatoes, tomato paste, anchovies, bay leaf, and salt and pepper to taste. Cover with stock and water. Simmer for approximately 35 to 45 minutes. Add more water if the sauce appears to be drying out. Remove bay leaf before serving.

Serve with spaghetti or pasta.

Makes 2 to 3 cups sauce.

Chapter 6

Pasta and Rice

Għaġin u Ross

Baked Macaroni in a Pastry Shell

Timpana

This is another recipe adapted from Gemma and Esther Said, owners of Gesters Restaurant, Xaghara, Gozo.

Ingredients

For the pastry:

pastry dough, enough for creating a top and bottom crust for an oblong casserole dish. See recipe page 273

For the filling:

1 large onion, peeled and chopped
2 cloves garlic, peeled and chopped
5 tablespoons olive oil
1 pound lean, ground beef or pork, or a combination of beef and pork
3 tablespoons tomato paste
1 to 2 fresh basil leaves, torn
1 teaspoon cumin seeds, crushed (optional)
1 teaspoon mixed spice (optional)
1 to 2 sprigs fresh Italian parsley, minced
1 large bay leaf
2 cups stock or water
1½ pounds cold cooked macaroni, such as penne or ziti
2 ounces freshly grated Parmesan cheese
2 hard-boiled eggs, shelled and chopped (optional)
3 eggs, well-beaten
salt and freshly ground pepper

Method

Preheat the oven to 350°F.

With a fork, pierce in several places pastry pie crust that has been placed in a well-floured, oblong casserole dish. Pre-bake bottom pie crust for approximately 10 minutes. Ceramic or metal weights can be placed over wax or parchment paper to prevent pie crust from bubbling. Remove from oven and cool. Set aside.

In a large skillet, sauté onion, and garlic in the olive oil until the onion becomes translucent, usually between 5 and 10 minutes. Add ground meat. Sauté until the meat turns pink. Remove from heat. Drain off and discard excess fat. Add tomato paste, basil leaves, cumin seeds, mixed spice, parsley, and bay leaf. Cover with stock or water. Simmer for approximately one hour, making certain that the sauce does not dry up. Remove and discard bay leaf. Set aside.

In a large bowl, carefully add meat and sauce mixture to the cooked macaroni. Add Parmesan cheese, chopped hard-boiled eggs, well-beaten eggs and salt and pepper to taste. Mix thoroughly.

Carefully pour macaroni mixture into the pastry-lined casserole dish. Place another piece of pastry on the top of the macaroni. Create vent holes in several places. Bake for one hour or until crust becomes golden brown.

Always a crowd pleaser, *Timpana* can be served either hot or cold.

6 to 8 servings.

Baked Macaroni

Mqarrun fil-Forn

Like timpana, this is a crowd pleaser but a lot less work on the cook! Leftovers (if there are any!) usually are quite welcome the following day. In our home, we make more than one casserole and freeze the other for use at another time.

Ingredients

1 large onion, peeled and chopped
1 to 2 cloves garlic, peeled and minced
2 tablespoons olive or other vegetable oil
1 pound lean ground sirloin or a combination of beef and pork (1 pound of sweet Italian sausage meat can be substituted)
2 cans (15 ounces each) tomato sauce or freshly prepared sauce
1 bay leaf
2 to 3 sprigs fresh Italian parsley, minced
1 to 2 large basil leaves, torn
1 rib celery, chopped
½ teaspoon crushed fennel seeds
salt and freshly ground pepper
2 cups cold water
1 cup vegetable or beef stock
2 eggs, well beaten (consider using: 1 egg plus 1 egg white)
1½ pounds cooked pasta such as ziti, penne, or rigatoni
freshly grated Parmesan cheese
several part-skim or whole-milk mozzarella slices

Method

Preheat the oven to 375° F.

In a large skillet, sauté onion and garlic in the olive oil until the onion becomes translucent, usually between 5 and 10 minutes. Add ground meat. Sauté until meat becomes pink. Remove from heat. Drain off and discard excess fat. Add tomato sauce, bay leaf, parsley, basil, celery, fennel seeds, and salt and pepper to taste. Cover with water and stock. Simmer for approximately 35 to 40 minutes until the sauce begins to thicken. Remove and discard bay leaf. Cool.

Crack eggs in a small dish. Add to sauce and quickly pour into the cooked macaroni. Mix thoroughly. Carefully pour mixture in a well-greased glass or ceramic casserole dish. Top with grated Parmesan cheese. Mozzarella slices also can be used as topping.

Bake for approximately 45 to 60 minutes, or until the top blackens a bit.

Serve hot. Leftovers can be refrigerated and reheated or eaten cold the following day. Many Maltese (myself included) like to nibble on this cold!

4 to 5 servings.

Stuffed Manicotti Shells

Injokki Mimlija

Although many Maltese families make their own pasta shells, prepared shells are much easier on the home chef!

Ingredients

14 (1 package) manicotti shells, partially cooked
non stick vegetable spray
2 cups whole milk or part skim ricotta
2 well beaten eggs (consider 1 egg plus 2 egg whites)
1 large onion, peeled and chopped
2 to 3 cloves garlic, peeled and minced
2 tablespoons olive or vegetable oil
1 pound lean ground sirloin or a combination of beef and pork (1 pound of sweet Italian sausage meat can be substituted)
3 cans (15 ounces each) tomato sauce
2 to 3 leaves fresh basil torn, or 1 tablespoon dried leaves, crushed
1 bay leaf
1 to 3 sprigs Italian parsley, minced
salt and freshly ground pepper
1 cup vegetable or beef stock
1 cup water
freshly grated Parmesan cheese

Method

Preheat the oven to 375° F.

Carefully line up pasta shells on the bottom of a casserole dish that has been spray with non-stick vegetable spray. Set aside.

In a medium size bowl, mix ricotta and eggs until smooth. Set aside and refrigerate until ready to use.

In a large skillet, sauté onion and garlic in the olive oil until the onion becomes translucent, usually between 5 and 10 minutes. Add ground meat and sauté until meat becomes pink. Remove from heat. Drain off and discard excess fat. Add tomato sauce, basil, bay leaf, parsley, and salt and pepper to taste. Cover with stock and water.

Simmer for approximately 35 to 40 minutes until the sauce begins to thicken. Remove and discard bay leaf. Cool.

Carefully pour ricotta and egg mixture into the sauce. Mix well. With a small spoon, fill each pasta tube with the sauce and ricotta mixture. Pour remaining mixture over the shells. Sprinkle with Parmesan cheese. Bake for approximately 35 to 45 minutes. If the sauce appears to be drying out, add water.

Serve piping hot with a salad. Leftovers can be refrigerated and reheated the following day.

4 to 6 servings.

Variations

Some Maltese families will add one or two slices of bacon to the sauce while it is cooking. Others will cook the meat and mix it with the ricotta and eggs and then stuff each pasta shell with the mixture. Grated Parmesan cheese and a freshly prepared tomato sauce would be carefully poured over the stuffed shells and Parmesan cheese sprinkled on it before baking.

Macaroni and Ricotta with Tomato Sauce

Mqarrun bl-Irkotta u z-Zalza tat-Tadam

This recipe, another family crowd pleaser, is adapted from Rosemary Grima, who lives in San Gwann, Malta.

Ingredients

1 pound whole-milk or part-skim ricotta
2 ounces milk
2 sprigs Italian parsley, chopped
salt and freshly ground pepper
1 pound cooked pasta such as penne or ziti, well drained
2 cups prepared tomato sauce (see recipes in chapter 5)

Method

In a large bowl, mix the ricotta, milk, and parsley. Season with salt and pepper. Add the cooked pasta and mix well. Transfer pasta and ricotta mixture to a large pasta dish. In the middle of the pasta, pour the sauce.

Serve hot.

3 to 4 servings.

Baked Rice 1

Ross fil-Forn 1

Some food historians believe ross fil-forn is a truly Maltese dish, dating back to the Phoenicians. Like timpana, ross fil-forn is a crowd pleaser and can be served either hot or cold. This recipe is adapted from Gemma and Esther Said, owners of Gesters Restaurant, Xaghara, Gozo.

Ingredients

1 onion, peeled and chopped
1 to 2 cloves garlic, peeled and minced
5 tablespoons olive or other vegetable oil
1 pound lean ground beef or pork, or combination of beef and pork
4 cups cold water
6 tablespoons tomato paste
2 to 3 leaves basil, shredded
1 to 2 sprigs fresh Italian parsley, minced
1 teaspoon mixed spice
salt and freshly ground pepper
4 eggs, well-beaten (consider using two eggs plus 2 egg whites)
freshly grated Parmesan cheese
1½ cups uncooked white rice

Method

Preheat the oven to 350°F.

In a large skillet, sauté the onion and garlic cloves in olive oil until the onion becomes translucent, usually between 5 and 10 minutes. Add ground meat. Sauté until the meat is cooked. Drain off and discard excess fat. Add water, tomato paste, basil, parsley, mixed spice, and salt and pepper to taste. Simmer for another 25 to 35 minutes. Stir thoroughly, making certain the meat is not in clumps. Cool. In a separate bowl, mix eggs and freshly grated Parmesan cheese. Add to meat mixture. Set aside.

Place uncooked rice in well-greased, oblong glass baking dish. Carefully ladle the ground meat mixture into the rice. Bake for 30 minutes. Remove baking dish from oven. Stir rice mixture thoroughly.

Return baking dish into oven for approximately one hour or until the top is browned. If the rice appears to be drying out too soon, add additional water and stir again.

Serve hot. Leftovers can be refrigerated and reheated or eaten cold the following day.

5 to 6 servings.

Variations

A handful of fresh or frozen peas can be included in the rice/meat mixture when it is removed for the oven for stirring. Many Maltese families in North America and in Malta, too, will use canned tomato sauce or canned tomatoes with less water instead of the tomato paste, which the recipe calls for. Some Maltese families also include shelled, chopped, hard-boiled eggs in their baked rice.

Baked Rice 2

Ross fil-Forn 2

This is an adaption of the original method that many cooks in Malta and in North America often use because the resulting casseroles can be frozen for use later. This is a family favorite in my brother's household and very easy to make.

Ingredients

1 large onion, peeled and chopped
1 to 2 cloves garlic, peeled and minced
4 to 5 tablespoons olive or other vegetable oil
1 pound lean ground sirloin
2 to 3 sprigs Italian parsley, minced
1 to 2 large leaves fresh basil, torn
1 bay leaf
salt and freshly ground pepper
4 cans (15 ounces each) tomato sauce
2 cups cold water
4 to 6 cups cooked, long grained white rice
2 large eggs, well beaten (consider using one egg plus one egg white)
2 tablespoons freshly grated Parmesan cheese
several slices of mozzarella or other cheese for topping (optional)

Method

Preheat the oven to 375°F.

In a large skillet, sauté chopped onion and garlic in olive oil until the onion becomes translucent, usually between 5 and 10 minutes. Add ground meat and cook until the meat is no longer pink. Drain excess fat and discard. Add parsley, basil, bay leaf, and salt and pepper to taste. Add tomato sauce. Cover with water. Simmer for approximately 40 minutes. Add more water if the sauce appears to be drying out. Remove from heat. Cool.

Place cooked rice in large bowl. Add sauce and well beaten eggs. Mix thoroughly. Carefully spoon rice/sauce mixture in a well-greased (no-stick spray is fine) casserole dish. Top with Parmesan cheese and mozzarella slices. Bake for approximately 45 minutes, until top starts to blacken.

Serve hot. Leftovers can be refrigerated and reheated or eaten cold the following day.

5 to 6 servings.

Variations

Italian sausage, with the casing removed, can be used with or substituted for the ground beef. This makes the sauce spicy. To obtain some of the "spiciness" without using pork, we use a teaspoon of crushed fennel seeds, plus 1 large sage leaf, crushed, and a sprig or so of fresh thyme.

Some families like to add ½ cup of freshly shelled or frozen peas to the sauce/rice mixture before baking. Other families add one cup of ricotta to the rice mixture before baking.

Papa's Maltese Rice

Ross fil-Forn ta' Missieri

In 1970, our local electric company sponsored a cooking competition, asking customers to submit their favorite low-cost recipes. This recipe was my mother's version of her father's favorite dish, and it won first prize. The cost of the ingredients for making this dish at the time: $2.35!

Ingredients

1 large onion, peeled and finely chopped
2 cloves garlic, peeled and minced
2 tablespoons olive oil
¾ pound lean, ground sirloin
¼ pound, casing removed, diced Italian sausage meat
2 sprigs Italian parsley, minced
½ rib celery, chopped
3 cans (8 ounces each) tomato sauce
2 tablespoons tomato paste
1 bay leaf
2 cups cold water
1½ cups uncooked long-grain white rice
several slices of mozzarella or other cheese for topping
3 tablespoons freshly grated Parmesan cheese

Method

Preheat the oven to 350°F.

In a large skillet, sauté chopped onion and garlic in olive oil until the onion becomes translucent, usually between 5 and 10 minutes. Add ground meat and sausage and cook until the meat is no longer pink. Drain off and discard excess fat. Add parsley, celery, tomato sauce, tomato paste, and bay leaf. Add cold water. Simmer until sauce begins to thicken, approximately 35 minutes. Remove and discard bay leaf. Cool and set aside.

Place uncooked rice in well-greased, oblong Pyrex dish. Carefully ladle the ground meat mixture into the rice and mix well. Bake for 30 minutes. Remove baking dish from oven. Stir rice mixture thoroughly.

Top with mozzarella and grated Parmesan cheese. Return baking dish into oven for approximately one hour or until the top is browned. Add more water and stir thoroughly if the sauce appears to be drying out. Remove from oven.

Serve hot. Leftovers can be refrigerated and reheated or eaten cold the following day.

5 to 6 servings.

Artichoke and Rice Pie

Torta ta l'Qaqoċċ u Ross

Ingredients

For the pastry:

pastry for a 9-inch double crust pie, see page 273
egg wash

For the filling:

1 large onion, peeled and chopped
2 tablespoons olive or other vegetable oil
6 to 8 artichoke hearts (rinsed and well-drained canned artichoke hearts can be used)
3 to 4 large, ripe tomatoes, peeled and chopped or 1 can (28 ounces) peeled tomatoes or purée
1 cup cold water
salt and freshly ground pepper
4 to 5 cups cooked, long-grain white rice
3 to 4 tablespoons freshly grated Parmesan cheese
2 eggs, well beaten (consider using 1 egg plus 1 egg white)

Method

Preheat the oven to 350°F.

Place a freshly rolled out pie crust on a well-floured pie plate. With a fork, pierce the crust in several places. Pre-bake bottom pie crust for approximately 10 minutes. Ceramic or metal weights can be placed over wax or parchment paper to prevent pie crust from bubbling. Remove from oven and cool. Set aside.

In a large skillet, sauté onion in olive oil until the onion becomes translucent, usually between 5 and 10 minutes. Add artichoke hearts, tomatoes, water, and salt and pepper to taste.

In a large bowl, combine artichoke mixture, rice, Parmesan cheese, and well beaten eggs. Mix thoroughly.

Carefully spoon filling into pastry-lined plate. Cover filling with top pastry. Seal and flute edges. Brush top crust with egg wash. Create vent holes in top crust. Bake for approximately 45 minutes, or until crust turns golden brown. Serve hot.

3 to 4 servings.

Rice with Ricotta

Ross bl-Irkotta

Ingredients

2 cups long-grain rice, cooked in vegetable or chicken stock, drained
2 cups whole milk or part-skim ricotta
½ stick unsalted butter or margarine, melted
4 eggs, well beaten (consider 2 eggs plus 2 egg whites)
4 to 5 sprigs Italian parsley, minced
salt and freshly ground pepper
2 to 4 tablespoons freshly grated Parmesan cheese
slices of mozzarella cheese (optional)

Method

Preheat the oven to 350°F.

In a large bowl, mix rice, ricotta, butter, and eggs. Add salt and pepper to taste and Parmesan cheese. Top with mozzarella slices.

Spoon mixture into a well-greased, Pyrex casserole or baking dish. Bake for approximately 35 to 45 minutes, or until the top begins to brown.

Serve either hot or cold.

4 servings.

Saffron Rice

Ross biz-Żagħfran

Ingredients

1 egg, well-beaten
3 to 4 threads saffron, or small packet saffron
3 tablespoons freshly grated Parmesan cheese
1 tablespoon unsalted butter or margarine
salt and freshly ground pepper
2 cups long-grain rice, cooked in chicken stock, drained
olive or other vegetable oil for pan frying

Method

In a large bowl, combine egg, saffron, grated cheese, butter, and salt and pepper with the cooked rice. Mix thoroughly. Heat olive oil In a large skillet. Carefully pour rice mixture, stirring all the while until the egg is set.

Serve hot.

3 to 4 servings.

Kitchen Notes

Many families, including mine, will add a few strands of saffron to their own tomato sauce as it is cooking. This is a wonderful addition to tomato sauce for pasta, spaghetti, or rice.

Ravioli

Ravjul

Ravjul traditionally were served on Fridays in Malta when eating meat was forbidden by the Catholic Church. Maltese ravjul differs from many Italian ravioli because semolina is used with the flour. Many Maltese families, however, will make the dish with regular flour instead.

Ingredients

For the dough:

3 cups all-purpose unbleached flour, sifted
1 cup semolina
1 teaspoon salt
ice water for binding

For the filling:

2 pounds whole-milk or part-skim ricotta
2 eggs (consider: 1 egg plus 1 egg white)
3 to 4 sprigs fresh Italian parsley, minced
salt and freshly ground pepper

Method

In a large bowl, sift together flour, semolina, and salt. Add ice water to bind. Wrap in plastic wrap and refrigerate for at least one hour.

In another bowl, mix ricotta, eggs, parsley, and salt and pepper to taste until smooth. Set aside.

On a marble board or other hard surface, roll out the dough. (If you have used semolina, this can be difficult.) Drop the ricotta mixture by the teaspoon across the dough in straight lines. Fold over, pinch closed, and separate using a sharp knife. Place individual ravioli in boiling water for approximately 20 minutes, or until the dough is tender.

Serve hot with plain tomato sauce or meat sauce.

3 to 4 servings.

Kitchen Notes

Freshly made ravjul can be frozen and used at a later date.

Chapter 7

Fish and Seafood

Ħut u Frott tal-Baħar

Snail Sauce

Zalza tal-Bebbux

Do not even think about using the slugs and snails found in your garden! Although as a child living in New York City I remember friends using snails that were packed in large burlap bags, today, packaged escargots are a smart choice. Look for them in either a specialty grocery or from one of the specialty mail-order companies listed in the resources section.

Ingredients

1 large onion, peeled and sliced
1 to 2 cloves garlic, peeled and minced
2 tablespoons olive or other vegetable oil
1 to 2 sprigs parsley, minced
1 can (8 ounces) tomato sauce
1 cup fish stock
1 dozen escargot, usually the contents of 1 can (3 ounces) drained and well rinsed under running cold water
one pound cooked pasta or spaghetti

Method

In a large skillet, sauté onion and garlic in olive oil until onion becomes translucent, usually between 5 and 10 minutes. Add parsley and salt and pepper. Cover with tomato sauce and stock and simmer for approximately 15 minutes, when sauce begins to thicken. Add snails and simmer for another 10 to 20 minutes, making certain the sauce does not dry out. Serve piping hot over pasta or spaghetti.

2 to 3 servings.

Kitchen Notes

One reason canned snails are preferred in many homes has as much to do with convenience as with odor. The odor of fresh snails cooking is intense. If fresh snails are used, make certain they are well cleaned. They should be put in the sauce with their shell. The snails are done when a skewer easily can remove the snail inside the shell.

Snails in Garlic Sauce

Bebbux bl-Aljoli

Ingredients

½ cup unseasoned bread crumbs
1 to 2 cloves garlic, peeled and minced
1 small, ripe tomato, chopped finely
5 to 6 sprigs Italian parsley, minced
salt and freshly ground pepper, to taste
4 to 5 tablespoons olive or other vegetable oil
2 tablespoons wine vinegar
1 dozen escargot, usually the contents of one 3-ounce can, drained and well rinsed under running cold water

Method

In a large bowl, mix bread crumbs, garlic, tomato, and parsley. Add salt and pepper. Carefully drizzle olive oil and vinegar over the mixture. Toss carefully. Chill for at least one hour.

Served this sauce over the cold, cooked snails.

2 to 3 servings.

Anchovy Fritters

Sfineġ ta' l-Inċova

Ingredients

For the batter:

1 cup sifted unbleached, all-purpose flour
squeeze of lemon
1 teaspoon baking powder
ice water
oil for deep frying

For the filling:

3½ to 5 ounces anchovies, chopped and rinsed several times under running cold water to reduce saltiness

Method

In a large bowl, sift flour and baking powder. Add a squeeze of lemon, plus ice water to make a stiff paste. Wrap in plastic wrap and chill in refrigerator for approximately one hour.

Dip anchovies pieces in batter. Carefully drop pieces in deep fryer. Remove when fritters turn golden. Drain anchovies fritters on absorbent paper.

Serve piping hot.

3 to 4 servings.

Variations

Boiled codfish also is used to make fritters (*Fritturi tal-bakkaljaw*). They can be made the same way, although salt usually is added when sifting the flour and baking powder.

Kitchen Notes

In Malta, fresh anchovies sometimes are available and used to make these fritters. Instead of deep frying, pan frying of the fritters also is possible and may be preferred by the more calorie-conscious.

Anchovy Pie

Torta ta' l-Inċova

Ingredients

For the pastry:

pastry for a 9-inch double crust pie, see page 273
egg wash

For the filling:

1 large onion, peeled and chopped
1 to 2 cloves garlic, peeled and minced
2 tablespoons olive or other vegetable oil
2 to 3 large ripe tomatoes, chopped or 1 can (28 ounces) peeled or crushed tomatoes
2 tablespoons capers, well drained and rinsed
3½ to 5 ounces flat anchovies, rinsed under cold running water, and well drained
10 to 12 pitted black olives, rinsed, well drained, and sliced
1 to 2 large sprigs mint, minced
salt and freshly ground pepper
3 cups fish or vegetable stock
1 pound spinach, well-rinsed, stems removed, steamed, and chopped
½ cup freshly shelled or frozen peas

Method

Preheat the oven to 350°F.

With a fork, pierce in several places bottom pie crust that has been placed in a well-floured pie plate. Pre-bake bottom pie crust for approximately 10 minutes. Ceramic or metal weights can be placed over wax or parchment paper to prevent pie crust from bubbling. Remove from oven and cool. Set aside.

In a large skillet, sauté onion and garlic in olive oil until onion becomes translucent, usually between 5 and 10 minutes. Add tomatoes, capers, anchovies, olives, mint, and salt and pepper. Cover with stock. Simmer for approximately 20 minutes, until tomatoes are tender. Remove from heat. Add spinach and peas. Simmer for another 10 minutes. Mix well. Cool.

Carefully place anchovy-spinach-pea mixture in precooked pastry-lined plate. Cover filling with top pastry. Seal and flute edges. Brush top crust with egg wash. Create vent holes in top crust. Bake for approximately 45 minutes, or until crust becomes golden brown.

Serve hot.

3 to 4 servings.

Kitchen Notes

Most cooks will forego the salt because of the anchovies, capers, and olives in the dish. This pie often is just referred to as *torta tal-ispinaci*, spinach pie.

Octopus Salad

Insalata tal-Qarnita

This recipe is adapted from chef Giovanni Bianco and his partner Karmanu Bianco, owners of the restaurant Grabiel, Marsascala, Malta.

Ingredients

1 to 2 pounds cooked, cut-up octopus, cold
2 cloves garlic, peeled and minced
olive oil and wine vinegar for tossing
2 sprigs shredded basil
1 to 2 sprigs Italian parsley, minced
1 to 2 sprigs mint, minced
1 to 2 sprigs marjoram
1 sprig oregano
2 cups cooked, cold spaghetti

For garnish:

julienne slices of carrot
toasted crusty bread dipped in olive oil

Method

In a large bowl, toss cut-up octopus pieces and other ingredients with cooked spaghetti. Garnish with julienne carrots.

Serve with dipped-in-olive oil, toasted Maltese or crusty bread.

3 to 4 servings.

Octopus Stew

Stuffat tal-Qarnita

Ingredients

1 large onion, peeled and chopped
1 to 2 cloves garlic, peeled and minced
2 tablespoons olive or other vegetable oil
2 pounds (approximately) cleaned, fresh octopus, sliced into small pieces or frozen octopus, thawed and chopped
3 to 4 large ripe tomatoes, chopped or 1 can (28 ounces) peeled or crushed tomatoes
2 tablespoons tomato paste
1 to 3 sprigs Italian parsley, minced
1 sprig fresh mint, minced or 1 tablespoon dried mint crushed
1 bay leaf
salt and freshly ground pepper
3 cups fish stock
5 cups cold water
1 cup white wine (optional)
10 pitted green olives, drained, well rinsed, and sliced
2 tablespoons capers, drained and well rinsed

Method

In a large skillet, sauté onion and garlic until onion becomes translucent, usually between 5 and 10 minutes. Add octopus pieces, tomatoes, tomato paste, parsley, mint, bay leaf, and salt and pepper. Cover with stock and water. Simmer for approximately 90 minutes, stirring occasionally to make certain stew does not dry out. Add wine, olives, and capers to the stew approximately 30 minutes before completion. Remove bay leaf before serving.

Serve hot.

3 to 4 servings.

Variations

Although *stuffat tal-qarnita* usually is served over spaghetti, many Maltese families will add two or three thinly sliced potatoes plus a cup of peas to the stew near the conclusion of cooking and skip the pasta.

Other families will include a handful of golden raisins (sultanas) before the conclusion of cooking.

Squid Stew

Stuffat tal-Klamari

Prepare octopus stew according to previous recipe, but replacing the octopus with 2 pounds of sliced, cleaned (ink bags removed) fresh or thawed squid.

Grilled Swordfish

Pixxispad Mixwi

Ingredients

4 swordfish fillets (thawed, frozen fillets can be substituted)
4 tablespoons olive or other vegetable oil
juice of one lemon
4 ounces wine vinegar or dry red wine
2 cloves garlic, peeled and minced
1 to 2 shallots, peeled and sliced
2 to 3 sprigs Italian parsley, minced
1 to 2 springs mint, minced
salt and freshly ground pepper

Method

Prepare grill.

In a large bowl, marinate the swordfish fillets in olive oil, lemon juice, vinegar or wine, garlic, shallots, parsley, mint, and salt and pepper. Refrigerate marinated fish for approximately 1 hour. Grill fillets for approximately 10 to 15 minutes, turning over as necessary.

Serve hot.

4 servings.

Mackerel Casserole

Stuffat tal-Kavalli

Ingredients

olive oil
3 large, potatoes, peeled, and thinly sliced
1 large onion, thinly sliced
3 large ripe tomatoes, thinly sliced
1 to 2 pounds mackerel, cleaned and sliced
juice from one lemon
1 to 2 sprigs Italian parsley, minced
salt and freshly ground pepper
3 to 4 cups fish stock or water with 2 tablespoons of tomato paste
1 large sprig mint, shredded

Method

Preheat the oven to 375°F.

Drizzle olive oil on the bottom of large casserole dish. Layer sliced potatoes, and then onions, and tomatoes on the bottom of dish. Place mackerel pieces on top of tomato pieces. Add squeeze of lemon, parsley, and salt and pepper to taste. Cover with stock and water. Bake for approximately 30 minutes. If the liquid starts to dry out, add more water. Sprinkle shredded mint and a drizzle of olive oil at the conclusion of baking.

Serve hot.

3 to 4 servings.

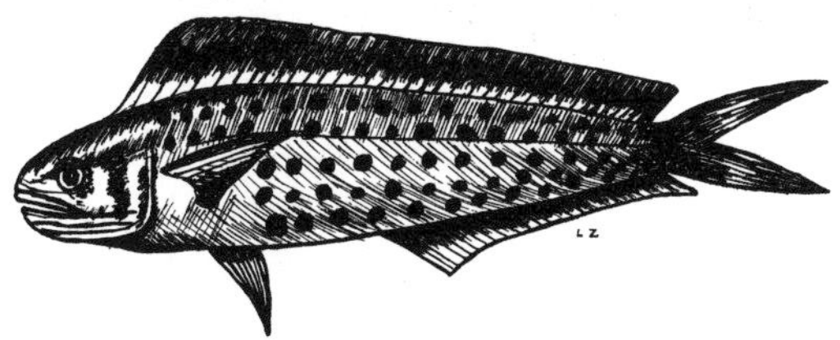

Lampuki with Wine Sauce

Lampuki biz-Zalza ta' l-Imbid

Ingredients

2 pounds *lampuki* or other fish, cleaned and sliced
flour for dredging
salt and freshly ground pepper
olive oil
1 large onion, peeled and chopped
1 to 1 cloves garlic, peeled and minced
2 to 3 sprigs Italian parsley, minced
1 to 2 sprigs fresh mint, minced
1 to 2 teaspoons fresh dill, chopped
2 cups cold water
2 cups fish stock
juice of ½ lemon
1 cup dry white wine
lemon slices for garnish

Method

Preheat the oven to 350°F.

In large, flat bottomed dish, dredge fish in flour seasoned with salt and pepper. Set aside.

Drizzle olive oil on the bottom of large casserole dish. Place fish in dish with onion and garlic. Add parsley, mint, and dill. Cover with water, stock, lemon juice, and wine. Bake for approximately 35 to 45 minutes, making certain to turn over fish at least once during cooking. If liquid starts to dry out, add more water. Garnish with lemon slices.

Serve hot.

3 to 4 servings.

Baked Lampuki and Potatoes

Lampuki bil-Patata fil-Forn

Although most people living in North America may not get the opportunity to savor lampuki unless they visit the Mediterranean region when it is in season, other available fish might be used in these traditional recipes.

Ingredients

olive or other vegetable oil
3 large potatoes, peeled and thinly sliced
1 large onion, peeled and sliced
3 to 4 large, ripe tomatoes, sliced
4 slices cleaned *lampuki* or other fish
2 to 3 sprigs Italian parsley, minced
1 to 2 cloves garlic, peeled and minced
10 green olives, drained, and well rinsed
2 to 3 cups cold water
2 to 3 cups fish stock
lemon slices

Method

Preheat oven to 350°F.

Drizzle olive oil on the bottom of casserole dish. Carefully layer potatoes on the bottom of the dish. Place onions and tomatoes over potatoes and then layer with fish. Add parsley, garlic, olives, and salt and pepper. Cover with water and stock. Bake for approximately 35 to 45 minutes, making certain to turn over fish at least once during cooking. If liquid starts to dry out, add more water. Garnish with lemon slices. Serve hot.

3 to 4 servings.

Kitchen Notes

This recipe works well with fish that has been filleted. Cooking time, however, needs to be reduced. The potatoes could remain in the oven for the additional time it takes for them to become tender.

Lampuki with Caper Sauce

Lampuki biz-Zalza tal-Kappar

Ingredients

4 slices *lampuki*, or other suitable fish
flour for dredging
salt and freshly ground pepper
1 large onion, peeled and sliced
2 tablespoons olive or other vegetable oil
3 large ripe tomatoes, chopped or 1 can (28 ounces) peeled tomatoes can be substituted
3 tablespoons capers, rinsed, and well drained
1 teaspoon vinegar
juice from one large lemon
2 cups fish stock
2 cups cold water
curly parsley for garnish
lemon slices

Method

Preheat the oven to 350°F.

Dredge sliced fish in flour seasoned with salt and pepper. Set aside.

In a large skillet, sauté onion in olive oil until onion becomes translucent, usually between 5 and 10 minutes. Add tomatoes, capers, vinegar, and lemon juice. Cover with stock and water. Simmer for approximately 20 minutes. Remove from heat. Cool.

Carefully place fish on the bottom of casserole dish. Cover with sauce. Bake for approximately 30 minutes. Turn fish over at least once. If liquid seems to be drying out, add more water. Garnish with parsley and lemon slices.

Serve hot.

3 to 4 servings.

Lampuki Pie

Torta tal-Lampuki

This is always a favorite that kindles fond memories for many Maltese who like to time their visits to Malta during "lampuki season." You might want to try this with another variety of fish.

Ingredients

For the pastry:

pastry for a 9-inch double crust pie, recipe page 273
egg wash

For the filling:

1 large onion, peeled and chopped
1 to 2 cloves garlic, peeled and minced
2 tablespoons olive oil
2 pounds *lampuki* or other suitable fish for baking
3 to 4 large ripe tomatoes, peeled and chopped or 1 can (28 ounces) peeled or crushed tomatoes
2 sprigs Italian parsley, minced
1 to 2 leaves basil, torn
10 green olives, drained, well-rinsed, chopped
½ cup golden raisins (sultanas) (optional)
salt and freshly ground pepper
1 medium size cauliflower, cut into florets, boiled, and drained
1 pound spinach, well-rinsed, stems removed, chopped, steamed, and drained

Method

Preheat the oven to 375°F.

Place a freshly rolled out pie crust on a well-floured pie plate. With a fork, pierce the crust in several places. Pre-bake bottom pie crust for approximately 10 minutes. Ceramic or metal weights can be placed over wax or parchment paper to prevent pie crust from bubbling. Remove from oven and cool. Set aside.

In a large skillet, sauté onion and garlic in olive oil until the onion becomes translucent, usually between 5 and 10 minutes. Add *lampuki*, tomatoes, parsley, basil, olives, raisins, and salt and pepper to taste. Simmer for approximately 15 minutes. Remove from heat. Add cauliflower florets and spinach. Mix well.

Carefully spoon *lampuki*/vegetable mixture into precooked pastry-lined plate. Cover filling with top pastry. Seal and flute edges. Brush top crust with egg wash. Create vent holes in top crust. Bake for approximately 45 minutes, or until the crust becomes golden brown.

3 to 4 servings.

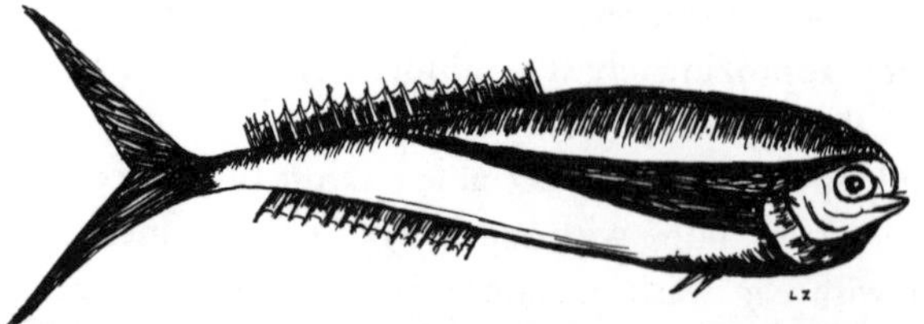

Tuna with Tomato Sauce and Wine

Tonn biz-Zalza tat-Tadam

Ingredients

4 thin slices fresh tuna
flour for dredging
salt and freshly ground pepper
1 large onion, peeled and chopped
1 to 2 cloves garlic, peeled and minced
2 tablespoons olive or other vegetable oil
4 large ripe tomatoes, chopped, peeled, and seeded or 1 can (28 ounces) peeled or crushed tomatoes
2 tablespoons tomato paste
juice from one half of a fresh lemon
2 tablespoons capers, drained, and well-rinsed
10 green olives, rinsed and chopped
2 to 3 anchovy fillets, drained, and well-rinsed
1 to 2 sprigs Italian parsley
salt and pepper
1 cup fish stock
2 cups cold water
1 cup dry white wine

Method

In a large, flat-bottomed dish, dredge tuna in flour seasoned with salt and pepper to taste. Set aside.

In a large skillet, sauté onion and garlic in olive oil until onion becomes translucent, usually between 5 and 10 minutes. Add tomatoes, tomato paste, lemon juice, capers, olives, anchovies, parsley, and salt and pepper to taste. Cover with stock and water. Simmer for 5 to

10 minutes. Carefully place tuna slices in sauce and simmer until tender, approximately 30 minutes. Add wine. Simmer for 10 to 15 minutes. Turn tuna slices over at least once, to insure proper cooking. If the sauce appears to be drying out, add water.

Serve either hot or cold.

3 to 4 servings.

Grilled Tuna

Tonn Mixwi

Ingredients

4 tuna steaks, cut thinly
olive or other vegetable oil for marinating
squeeze of one fresh lemon
1 to 2 sprigs fresh mint, minced
1 to 2 large shallots, peeled and minced or 1 medium size onion, peeled and minced
1 to 2 cloves garlic, peeled and minced
1 to 2 sprigs Italian parsley, minced
1 teaspoon fresh marjoram, minced
½ cup red wine vinegar or dry red wine
salt and freshly ground pepper
lemon wedges
loaf of crusty bread

Method

In a large bowl, marinate the tuna steaks in olive oil, lemon juice, mint, shallots, garlic, parsley, marjoram, vinegar or wine, and salt and pepper to taste. Refrigerate marinated fish for approximately 1 hour.

Prepare grill.

Grill the tuna on both sides. Baste as necessary with remaining marinade. Garnish with lemon wedges.

Serve hot or chilled with crusty bread, slices of fresh, ripe tomatoes, or a salad.

3 to 4 servings.

Baked Tuna

Tonn fil-Forn

Ingredients

4 thick slices of fresh tuna (frozen and thawed tuna may be substituted)

For marinade:

12 tablespoons olive or other vegetable oil, divided
juice from 1 lemon
6 tablespoons red wine vinegar or white wine
1 to 2 sprigs Italian parsley, minced
1 to 2 sprigs fresh mint, minced
1 to 2 cloves garlic, peeled and minced
2 to 3 shallots, peeled and chopped (1 medium onion can be substituted)
dash dry mustard powder (optional)
salt and freshly ground black pepper
curly parsley for garnish
lemon slices for garnish

Method

Preheat the oven to 350°F.

Combine the tuna, 10 tablespoons olive oil, lemon juice, vinegar, parsley, mint, garlic, shallots, mustard powder, and salt and pepper to taste. Refrigerate at least one hour.

Drizzle 2 tablespoons olive oil on the bottom of a casserole dish. Carefully place tuna slices in the dish and cover with marinade. Bake for approximately 35 to 45 minutes, until tuna is thoroughly cooked. Turn over the tuna at least once. Add water if the marinade begins to dry out. Garnish with curly parsley and lemon slices.

Serve hot.

3 to 4 servings.

Tuna Pie

Torta tat-Tonn

Ingredients

For the pastry:

pastry for a 9-inch double crust pie, recipe page 273
egg wash

For the filling:

1 large onion, peeled and chopped
1 to 2 cloves garlic, peeled and minced
2 tablespoons olive or other vegetable oil
3 large ripe tomatoes, peeled and chopped or 1 can (28 ounces) peeled or crushed tomatoes
1 large Italian frying pepper, seeded and chopped
10 to 12 pitted green olives
salt and freshly ground pepper
2 to 3 tuna steaks (free of bones), sliced
2 cups fish stock or water

Method

Place a freshly rolled out pie crust on a well-floured pie plate. With a fork, pierce the crust in several places. Pre-bake bottom pie crust for approximately 10 minutes. Ceramic or metal weights can be placed over wax or parchment paper to prevent pie crust from bubbling. Remove from oven and cool. Set aside.

In a large skillet, sauté onion and garlic in olive oil until the onion becomes translucent, usually between 5 and 10 minutes. Add tomatoes, frying pepper, olives, and salt and pepper to taste. Add the tuna steaks. Cover with stock and simmer the mixture for approximately 15 minutes.

Carefully spoon tuna and vegetable mixture in precooked pastry-lined plate. Cover filling with top pastry. Seal and flute edges. Brush top crust with egg wash. Create vent holes in top crust. Bake for approximately 45 minutes, or until the crust becomes golden brown.

Serve piping hot.

3 to 4 servings.

Variations

In a pinch, I have used three cans (6 ounces each) of tuna. If you decided to do that, there is no need to pre-cook the tuna before placing it into the pie.

Tuna or Swordfish Salad

Insalata tat-Tonn jew Pixxispad

Ingredients

3 ounces pickled onions
1 large onion, peeled and chopped or 3 large shallots, chopped
2 to 3 tablespoons capers, well-drained and rinsed
3 to 4 tablespoons green olives, well-drained and rinsed
2 hard-boiled eggs, shelled, peeled, and chopped
3 to 4 large potatoes, peeled, boiled, chilled, and sliced
2 to 3 baked swordfish or tuna steaks, deboned, flaked, and chilled
salt and freshly ground pepper
lettuce wedges for four persons
olive oil and vinegar for drizzling or vinaigrette
3 to 4 large ripe tomatoes, sliced
lemon wedges
loaf of crusty bread

Method

In large bowl, toss pickled onion, onion, capers olives, hard-boiled eggs, and potatoes. Add fish. Toss again. Add salt and pepper to taste. Place each of four portions of the fish salad on a lettuce wedge. Drizzle with olive oil and vinegar. Garnish with tomatoes slices and lemon wedges. Refrigerate until ready to use.

Serve well-chilled with a loaf of crusty bread.

4 servings.

Swordfish with Caper Sauce

Pixxispad biz-Zalza tal-Kappar

Ingredients

4 swordfish steaks
olive or other vegetable oil
1 small onion, peeled and sliced
salt and freshly ground pepper

For the sauce:

See recipe for Caper Sauce, page 135.

Method

Prepare grill.

In a large flat bottomed plate, coat both sides of the swordfish with oil. Place on grill with the onions. Sprinkle with salt and pepper. Grill until the swordfish is tender turning over as necessary. Remove from grill. Serve with the caper sauce.

3 to 4 servings.

Baked Fish Casserole

Ħut Mimli l-Forn

Ingredients

olive oil
2 large potatoes, peeled and thinly sliced
2 large onions, peeled and sliced
1 cup unseasoned bread crumbs
1 to 2 cloves garlic, peeled and minced
1 large shallot, peeled and minced
1 tablespoon of butter or unsalted margarine
1 sprig fresh dill weed
salt and freshly ground pepper
1 pound cleaned, boned fish such as tuna, sliced
2 well beaten eggs (consider 1 egg plus 1 egg white)
2 to 3 large tomatoes, sliced
1 tablespoon capers, drained and well rinsed
approximately 10 pitted green olives, chopped
2 cups fish stock or water
curly parsley
lemon wedges

Method

Drizzle olive oil on the bottom of a casserole dish. Carefully place a layer of potato slices in casserole and top with a layer of onion slices. Set aside.

In a flat-bottomed dish mix bread crumbs, garlic, shallot, butter, dill weed, and salt and pepper to taste. Set aside.

Dunk fish slices in well-beaten eggs and coat with bread crumb mixture. Place fish slices in casserole dish. Top with tomato slices, capers, and olives. Cover with stock. Bake for approximately 35 to 45 minutes, until fish is thoroughly cooked. Turn the fish over at least once. Add water to the sauce if it begins to dry out. Garnish with curly parsley and lemon wedges.

Serve hot or cold.

4 servings.

Chapter 8

Meats

Laħam

Beef Olives

Braġjoli

This recipe is adapted from sisters Gemma and Esther Said, owners of Gesters Restaurant, Xaghra, Gozo.

Ingredients

½ pound lean ground beef or pork or a combination of beef and pork
1 large onion, peeled and chopped
2 to 4 cloves garlic, peeled and chopped
1 to 2 sprigs Italian parsley, chopped
1 sprig marjoram
salt and freshly ground pepper
2 tablespoons olive or other vegetable oil
2 hard-boiled eggs, shelled and chopped
4 slices thin steak
1 cup red wine

Method

Preheat the oven to 350° F.

In a large skillet, sauté the ground meat with ½ of the chopped onion and ½ of the garlic, parsley, marjoram, and salt and pepper to taste in olive oil until the meat is pink. Remove from heat. Drain off and discard excess fat. Cool. Add chopped hard-boiled eggs. Carefully place ground meat mixture in individual steak strips. Roll-up and tie securely with kitchen twine. Place in casserole dish. Add red wine and remaining chopped onion and garlic. Simmer for approximately 20 minutes, making certain the liquid does not dry out.

Serve hot, surrounded by boiled potatoes or other vegetables.

4 servings.

Beef Olives Stuffed with Ricotta and Spinach

Braġjoli Mimlijin bl-Irkotta u l'Ispinaċi

Ingredients

1 cup whole-milk or part-skim ricotta
1 pound spinach, well-rinsed, stems removed, steamed, and chopped
1 egg, well beaten
2 to 3 sprigs Italian parsley, minced
dash nutmeg
1 teaspoon fresh dill weed, chopped (optional)
2 tablespoons freshly grated Parmesan cheese
salt and freshly ground pepper
4 thin braggoli steaks, pounded
2 cups crushed tomatoes
2 cups dry red wine
boiled potatoes or other vegetables

Method

Preheat oven to 350°F.

In a large bowl, mix ricotta, spinach, egg, parsley, nutmeg, dill weed, Parmesan cheese, and salt and pepper. Carefully place ricotta mixture in individual steak strips. Roll-up and tie securely with kitchen twine. Place in casserole dish. Add tomatoes and red wine. Simmer for approximately 20 minutes, making certain the liquid does not dry up.

Serve surrounded by boiled potatoes or other vegetables.

4 servings.

Meat Loaf

Pulpettun

Ingredients

1½ pounds lean ground beef or a combination of beef and pork
½ cup unseasoned bread crumbs
1 large onion, peeled and chopped
2 to 3 cloves garlic, peeled and minced
2 to 3 sprigs Italian parsley, minced
1 to 2 sprigs fresh thyme
1 to 2 leaves sage, crushed
leaves from 1 to 2 sprigs fresh rosemary, crushed
1 to 2 sprigs fresh marjoram, crushed
salt and freshly ground pepper
1 egg, well beaten
1 hard-boiled egg, shelled
1 to 2 slices lean bacon (optional)

Method

Preheat the oven to 350°F.

In a large bowl, combine ground meat, bread crumbs, onion, garlic, parsley, thyme, sage, rosemary, marjoram, and salt and pepper to taste. Add well beaten egg and mix well. Put meat mixture in a meatloaf pan. Carefully insert the whole, shelled, hard-boiled egg inside the meatloaf. Place bacon slices on top. Bake for approximately 35 to 45 minutes, or until the meat is barely pink. Each slice should have the hard cooked egg in its center.

Serve hot or cold.

4 servings.

Kitchen Notes

To reduce some of the fat in the recipe, use a double meatloaf baking dish, available in the kitchen department of many large department stores or from specialty kitchenware shops. The fat drips from the first baking dish into the one directly beneath it. The liquid fat then can be discarded.

Several of the older, more traditional recipes for *pulpettun* call for the use of brain, pork livers, plus a special lace-like strip of fat—*caul*—to encase the meatloaf. Caul, which can be either pork or sheep fat, often is used in French cooking. Traditional recipes for *Pulpetti*, Maltese meatballs, made use of brain and sweetbreads. This is no longer done.

Another way *pulpettun* can be prepared is by covering and tying the chopped meat mixture in muslin, and then boiling it in a vegetable-based soup. After cooking, the muslin is unwrapped and the meatloaf is served with the vegetables from the soup.

Roast Beef

Ċanga fil-Forn

Many Maltese families have fond memories of large Sunday gatherings with either a beef or pork roast, and with a side dish of timpana. It just wouldn't be Sunday without it!

Ingredients

vegetable oil or vegetable shortening
1 to 2 large onions, peeled and chopped
1 clove garlic, peeled and minced
3 large potatoes, peeled and thinly sliced
1 eye round, bottom round, or silverside roast, approximately 5 to 7 pounds
3 to 4 sprigs Italian parsley, minced
1 to 2 sprigs fresh rosemary or 2 teaspoons dried rosemary
1 to 2 tablespoons freshly snipped chives, minced or one green or spring onion, finely sliced
salt and freshly ground pepper

Method

Preheat the oven to 350°F.

Grease a large roasting pan with shortening or vegetable oil. Carefully layer chopped onions and minced garlic in the pan. Follow with a layer of potatoes. Place roast on top of potatoes. Sprinkle the roast and potatoes with parsley, rosemary, chives, and salt and pepper to taste. Bake for at least 3 hours or until the roast is done. Turn over potatoes at least twice to make certain they are well cooked. Use a meat thermometer to make certain the roast is completely cooked. Remove potatoes from the oven, and drain on absorbent paper.

Serve either hot or cold with the pan-roasted potatoes and another vegetable.

4 to 6 servings.

Kitchen Notes

If the potatoes are not cooked when the meat is done, put them back in the oven, covered with foil, for another 10 minutes.

Steamed Meat

Laħam fuq il-Fwar

Alfred Grech remembers his mother making this in their Qormi home. As other friends remembered also, it was not uncommon for the beef to be steamed on the plate while a soup was simmering below.

Ingredients

3 to 4 tablespoons olive oil or vegetable shortening
1 large potato, peeled and very thinly sliced
4 thin strips of beef
1 to 2 cloves garlic, peeled and minced
1 to 2 sprigs Italian parsley, minced
1 to 2 sprigs fresh mint, minced
1 small leek, washed and chopped finely (optional)
salt and freshly ground pepper

Method

Drizzle olive oil on an ordinary kitchen plate. If using vegetable shortening, smear it on the plate. Place the very thin potato slices on top of the oil. Cover with beef strips. Season with garlic, parsley, mint, leeks, and salt and pepper to taste. Using potholders, carefully place the plate on top of a kettle of simmering water or soup. Keep in place approximately 1 to 1½ hours, or until the meat is completely steam-cooked.

Serve with vegetables or the soup simmering below the steamed meat.

3 to 4 servings.

Variations

Some Maltese families also cook thin pork chops *(kustilji tal-majjal fuq il-fwar)* this way.

Kitchen Notes

If you do not wish to use a kitchen plate for the steaming, a *Bain Marie*, used for steaming, is recommended.

Pork Olives

Braġjoli tal-Majjal

Ingredients

½ pound lean ground beef or pork or a combination
1 large onion, peeled and chopped
2 to 3 cloves garlic, peeled and chopped
1 teaspoon fennel seeds, crushed
1 to 2 leaves sage, crushed
1 to 2 sprigs thyme, crushed
1 to 3 sprigs Italian parsley, minced
1 to 2 sprigs marjoram, minced
salt and freshly ground pepper
2 tablespoons olive or other vegetable oil
2 hard-boiled eggs, shelled, sliced, and crumbled
4 slices pork (pork cutlets work well), pounded and flattened
1 cup white wine

Method

Preheat the oven to 350°F.

Sauté the ground meat with ½ of the chopped onion and ½ of the garlic, fennel seeds, sage, thyme, parsley, marjoram and salt and pepper to taste in olive oil until the meat is pink. Remove from heat. Drain off and discard excess fat. Cool. Add chopped, shelled,hard-boiled eggs. Carefully place ground meat mixture in individual pork strips. Roll-up and tie securely with kitchen twine. Place in casserole dish. Add wine and remaining chopped onion and garlic. Simmer for approximately 20 minutes, making certain the liquid does not dry out.

Serve hot, surrounded by boiled potatoes or other vegetables.

3 to 4 servings.

Kitchen Notes

Unseasoned bread crumbs may be substituted for part of the ground meat or they may be used instead of the ground meat. If substituting bread crumbs for ground meat, sauté onion and garlic in olive oil until the onion becomes translucent, usually between 5 and 10 minutes and then add to approximately one cup of bread crumbs that have been rubbed with 2 tablespoons of unsalted butter. Add seasonings and continue with the recipe.

Pork Stew

Stuffat tal-Majjal

Ingredients

1 pound lean pork, cut into one-inch cubes for stewing
flour for dredging
1 large onion, peeled and chopped
2 tablespoons olive or other vegetable oil
3 large tomatoes, chopped and seeded, or 1 can (28-ounces) peeled or crushed tomatoes
2 tablespoons tomato paste
3 to 4 cups cold water
2 cups vegetable stock
2 to 3 fresh or dried sage leaves, crushed
2 to 3 sprigs thyme, crushed
½ teaspoon mixed spice (optional)
salt and freshly ground pepper
1 cup freshly shelled or frozen peas

Method

In large flat-bottomed plate, dredge cubed pork in flour. Set aside.

In large saucepot, sauté onion in olive oil until the onion becomes translucent, usually between 5 and 10 minutes. Add pork. Simmer for approximately 15 minutes, when it begins to brown. Remove from heat. Drain and discard excess fat. Add tomatoes, tomato paste, water, stock, sage, thyme, mixed spice, and salt and pepper to taste. Simmer for approximately 45 minutes, or until the pork is thoroughly cooked. Add peas in the last 10 minutes of simmering.

3 to 4 servings.

Baked Pork Chops and Potatoes

Kustilji tal-Majjal bil-Patata l-Forn

Ingredients

4 thin pork chops
flour for dredging
2 to 3 large ripe tomatoes, sliced
3 to 4 large potatoes, peeled and thinly sliced
1 to 2 large onions, peeled and sliced
1 teaspoon fennel seeds. crushed
1 to 2 sprigs fresh thyme, crushed
2 to 3 fresh or dried sage leaves, crushed
salt and freshly ground pepper
2 cups vegetable or beef stock

Method

Preheat the oven to 350°F.

In large flat-bottomed dish, dredge pork chops in flour. Set aside.

In large casserole dish, layer in this order: ½ of the tomatoes, ½ of the potatoes, and ½ of the onions. Carefully place the pork chops over the onions. Sprinkle fennel seeds, thyme, sage, and salt and pepper to taste over pork chops. Place the remaining tomatoes, potatoes and onions in layers over the pork chops. Cover with stock. Bake for approximately 45 minutes to 1 hour, or until the chops are tender and the potatoes are cooked. Add water if the liquid appears to be drying up.

4 servings.

Variations

Dry white wine can be substituted for the stock. The pork chops also can be breaded.

Stuffed Pork Flank

Falda tal-Majjal Mimlija

Ingredients

2 pounds thick pork flank (rump), with a pocket

For the stuffing:

¾ pound lean ground beef or a combination of beef and ground pork
1 cup unseasoned bread crumbs
1 small onion or shallot, peeled and minced
1 to 2 sprigs Italian parsley, minced
1 to 2 sprigs fresh mint, minced
salt and freshly ground pepper
1 well beaten egg

Method

Preheat the oven to 350°F.

For the stuffing:

In a medium size bowl, combine ground meat, bread crumbs, onion, parsley, mint, salt and pepper, and egg.

Carefully stuff the flank pocket with the mixture. Using kitchen thread, sew the pocket closed. Carefully place pork in a kettle of boiling water or soup. Reduce heat and simmer for approximately 90 minutes. Remove from heat. Cool. Remove kitchen thread. Slice.

Serve with vegetables or soup.

3 to 4 servings.

Pork Roast

Majjal fil-Forn

Ingredients

vegetable oil or vegetable shortening
1 to 2 large onions, chopped
1 clove garlic, minced
2 to 3 large potatoes, peeled and thinly sliced
1 pork roast, approximately 5 to 7 pounds
1 to 2 sprigs Italian parsley, minced
1 to 2 teaspoons crushed fennel seeds
1 to 2 sprigs fresh thyme
3 fresh or dried sage leaves
2 tablespoons freshly snipped chives or one green or spring onion, finely sliced
salt and freshly ground pepper

Method

Preheat the oven to 350°F.

Grease a large roasting pan with shortening or vegetable oil. Carefully layer chopped onions and minced garlic in the pan. Follow with a layer of potatoes. Place roast on top of potatoes. Sprinkle the roast and potatoes with parsley, crushed fennel seeds, thyme, sage, chives, and salt and pepper to taste. Bake for at least 3 hours or until the roast is done. Turn over potatoes at least twice to make certain they are well cooked. Use a meat thermometer to make certain the roast is completely cooked. Remove potatoes from the oven, and drain on absorbent paper.

Serve either hot or cold with the pan-roasted potatoes and another vegetable.

4 to 6 servings.

Kitchen Notes

If the potatoes are not cooked when the pork is done, put them back in the oven, covered with foil, for another 10 minutes.

Lamb Stew

Stuffat tal-Ħaruf

Ingredients

1½ to 2 pounds lamb, cut into one-inch cubes for stewing
flour for dredging
1 large onion, peeled and chopped
2 to 3 cloves garlic, peeled and minced
2 tablespoons olive or other vegetable oil
3 large potatoes, peeled and sliced
2 to 3 carrots, peeled and sliced
½ teaspoon mixed spice (optional)
1 to 2 sprigs Italian parsley, minced
1 large bay leaf
salt and freshly ground pepper
3 cups vegetable or beef stock
5 cups cold water
1 cup freshly shelled or frozen peas

Method

In a large flat-bottom plate, dredge lamb in flour. Set aside.

In a large saucepot, sauté onion and garlic in olive oil until the onion becomes translucent, usually between 5 and 10 minutes. Add lamb and sauté for approximately 5 minutes. Add potatoes, carrots, mixed spice, parsley, bay leaf, and salt and pepper to taste. Cover with water and stock. Simmer for approximately 25 to 30 minutes or until the lamb is cooked and the vegetables are tender. Add peas at the conclusion of cooking. Remove bay leaf before serving.

Serve with rice or pasta.

3 to 4 servings.

Rabbit with Garlic and Wine

Fenek bit-Tewm u bl-Imbid

This recipe is adapted from Tony Scerri, owner and the chef at Bobbylands Restaurant, Dingli Cliffs, Malta.

Ingredients

1 rabbit (approximately 2 to 3 pounds), fresh or frozen, cut in pieces
olive or other vegetable oil suitable for frying
2 spring onions, chopped
4 to 5 cloves garlic, peeled and minced
2 sprigs mint, chopped
1 sprig thyme, minced
1 sprig marjoram, minced
3 sprigs Italian parsley, minced
salt and freshly ground pepper
2 cups red wine
3 large potatoes, peeled and sliced thinly

Method

In a large skillet, pan fry the rabbit in the olive oil with onion, garlic, mint, thyme, marjoram, parsley, and salt and pepper to taste for approximately 10 minutes, turning the pieces over frequently. Add the wine and sliced potatoes. Simmer for approximately 25 minutes, until the potatoes are soft. If the sauce appears to be drying out, add water.

Serve with spaghetti.

3 to 4 servings.

Kitchen Notes

Rabbit is traditionally served with either rice or spaghetti plus sauce in most Maltese homes.

Rabbit in Tomato Sauce

Fenek biz-Zalza tat-Tadam

Ingredients

1 large onion, peeled and chopped
2 to 3 cloves of garlic, peeled and minced
2 tablespoons olive or other vegetable oil
1 rabbit (approximately 2 to 3 pounds), fresh or frozen, cut in pieces
3 to 4 large ripe tomatoes, peeled, chopped, and seeded or 1 can (28 ounces) peeled or crushed tomatoes
2 to 3 basil leaves, torn
1 to 2 sprigs Italian parsley, minced
salt and freshly ground pepper
3 cups vegetable or chicken stock
3 cups cold water

Method

In a large skillet, sauté onion and garlic in olive oil until the onion becomes translucent, usually between 5 and 10 minutes. Add rabbit pieces, tomatoes, basil, parsley, and salt and pepper to taste. Cover with stock and water. Simmer for approximately 45 minutes or until the rabbit is tender.

Serve with spaghetti or rice.

3 to 4 servings.

Rabbit Stew

Stuffat tal-Fenek

Ingredients

2 large onions, peeled and chopped
2 to 3 cloves garlic, peeled and minced
2 tablespoons olive or other vegetable oil
1 rabbit (approximately 2 to 3 pounds) fresh or frozen, cut in pieces
2 carrots, peeled and sliced
1 bay leaf
salt and freshly ground pepper
3 cups vegetable or chicken stock
3 cups cold water
1 cup freshly shelled or frozen peas

Method

In a large skillet, sauté onion and garlic in olive oil until the onion becomes translucent, usually between 5 and 10 minutes. Add rabbit pieces, carrots, bay leaf, and salt and pepper to taste. Cover with stock and water. Simmer for approximately 45 minutes until rabbit is tender. Add peas at conclusion of cooking. Remove bay leaf before serving.

Serve with spaghetti or rice.

3 to 4 servings.

Curried Rabbit

Fenek bil-Curry

Ingredients

1 large onion, peeled and chopped
2 to 4 cloves garlic, peeled and minced
2 tablespoons olive or other vegetable oil
3 large potatoes, peeled and sliced
2 carrots, peeled and sliced
1 rabbit (approximately 2 to 3 pounds) fresh or frozen, cut in pieces
1 to 2 sprigs Italian parsley, minced
1 to 2 teaspoons curry powder
salt and freshly ground pepper
3 cups vegetable or chicken stock
2 cups cold water
½ cup freshly shelled or frozen peas
2 to 3 cups cooked, long-grain white rice

Method

In a large skillet, sauté onion and garlic in olive oil until the onion becomes translucent, usually between 5 and 10 minutes. Add potatoes, carrots, rabbit, parsley, curry powder, and salt and pepper to taste. Cover with stock and water. Simmer until vegetables and rabbit are tender. Turn over the rabbit during cooking. Add peas at conclusion of cooking. Add water if the liquid appears to be drying out.

Serve with boiled rice.

3 to 4 servings.

Kitchen Notes

Most Maltese cooks prefer Indian style curry powders, not Jamaican style curry powders. The choice is yours.

Rabbit with Black Olives and Capers

Fenek biż-Żebbuġ Iswed u l-Kappar

Ingredients

1 large onion, peeled and chopped
2 to 3 cloves garlic, peeled and minced
2 tablespoons olive or other vegetable oil
1 rabbit (approximately 2 to 3 pounds) fresh or frozen, cut in pieces
3 to 4 large ripe tomatoes, peeled, chopped, and seeded or 1 can (28 ounces) peeled or crushed tomatoes
1 cup black olives, pitted and sliced
3 tablespoons capers, rinsed and well drained
2 cups vegetable or chicken stock
2 cups cold water
salt and freshly ground pepper
1 cup dry white wine

Method

Preheat the oven to 350°F.

In a large skillet, sauté onions and garlic in olive oil until the onion becomes translucent, usually between 5 and 10 minutes. Add rabbit pieces, tomatoes, olives, capers, stock, water, and salt and pepper to taste. Simmer for another 15 minutes. Remove from heat. Add wine. Place rabbit mixture in casserole dish. Bake for approximately 30 to 45 minutes, turning rabbit pieces occasionally until the rabbit is cooked. If liquid appears to be drying out, add water.

Serve piping hot with spaghetti or rice.

3 to 4 servings.

Rabbit Pie

Torta tal-Fenek

Ingredients

For the pastry:

pastry for a 9-inch double crust pie, see page xx
egg wash

For the filling:

1 large onion, peeled and chopped
2 cloves garlic, peeled and minced
2 tablespoons olive or other vegetable oil
1 rabbit (approximately 2 to 3 pounds), fresh or thawed, cut into pieces
3 to 4 large ripe tomatoes, peeled, seeded, and chopped, or 1 can (28 ounces) peeled or crushed tomatoes
2 tablespoons tomato paste
dash mixed spice (optional)
1 bay leaf
salt and freshly ground pepper
1 cup vegetable or chicken stock
1 cup cold water
1 cup freshly shelled or frozen peas

Method

Preheat the oven to 375°F.

Place a freshly rolled out pie crust on a well-floured pie plate. With a fork, pierce the crust in several places. Pre-bake bottom pie crust for approximately 10 minutes. Ceramic or metal weights can be placed over wax or parchment paper to prevent pie crust from bubbling. Remove from oven and cool. Set aside.

In a large skillet, sauté onion and garlic in olive oil until the onion becomes translucent, usually between 5 and 10 minutes. Add rabbit, tomatoes, tomato paste, mixed spice, bay leaf, and salt and pepper to taste. Cover with stock and water. Simmer for approximately 20 minutes. Remove from heat. Cool. Carefully remove and discard all bones from the rabbit and return the meat to the mixture. Remove and discard bay leaf. Add peas and simmer for another 10 minutes minutes. Add more water if the mixture appears to be drying out. Remove from heat. Cool.

Carefully spoon rabbit and vegetable mixture in pastry-lined plate. Cover filling with top pastry. Seal and flute edges. Brush top crust with egg wash. Create vent holes in top crust. Bake for approximately 45 minutes, or until the crust becomes golden.

Serve piping hot.

3 to 4 servings.

Variations

Several pieces of pork are sometimes cooked with the rabbit and then added to the pie. Some families will add two well-beaten eggs to the mixture, prior to pouring it into the pie shell. It also is possible to add 1 to 2 potatoes (boiled and sliced) to the filling before baking.

Chopped Meat Pie

Torta tal-Kapuljat

Ingredients

For the pastry:

pastry for one 9-inch, double crust pie, see page 273
egg wash

For the filling:

1 to 2 large onions, diced
1 to 2 cloves garlic, peeled and minced
2 tablespoons olive or other vegetable oil
1 pound lean, chopped beef or combination of chopped pork
1 to 2 sprigs parsley, minced
1/8 teaspoon mixed spice (optional)
salt and freshly ground pepper
1 pound spinach, well-rinsed, shredded, steamed, and drained
1 egg plus one egg white, well-beaten
½ cup freshly shelled or frozen peas

Method

Preheat the oven to 375°F.

Place a freshly rolled out pie crust on a well-floured pie plate. With a fork, pierce the crust in several places. Pre-bake bottom pie crust for approximately 10 minutes. Ceramic or metal weights can be placed over wax or parchment paper to prevent pie crust from bubbling. Remove from oven and cool. Set aside.

In large saucepot, sauté onion and garlic until the onion becomes translucent, usually between 5 and 10 minutes. Add chopped meàt, parsley, mixed spice, and salt and pepper to taste. Simmer until the meat is cooked or becomes light pink. Drain off and discard excess fat. Cool. Add spinach, beaten egg, and peas. Mix well. Carefully spoon filling in pastry-lined plate.

Cover filling with top pastry. Seal and flute edges. Brush top crust with egg wash. Create vent holes in top crust. Bake for approximately 45 minutes, or until crust becomes golden brown.

Serve piping hot.

3 to 4 servings.

Variations

Many Maltese families like to add a slice of bacon and a shelled, chopped, hard-boiled egg to the mixture before baking. In some families, the spinach, peas, and egg are omitted.

Meat Pie 1

Torta tal-Laħam 1

Two Gozotian friends, one a senior citizen and the another a contemporary, remember this dish fondly. Another friend writes: "Mother made her meat pie using layers of canned corned beef and a mixture of peas and carrots, peeled potatoes and pie crust. It was my favorite dish at 'Ave Maria' house at Triq Santu Wistin, Zejtun, where we lived. What memories! My mother's version was the proletarian working family 'torta tal-laham fil-forn'. With six boys around, my mother had to make do with corned beef (we called it 'bulibif') in place of the more expensive stewing meat or pork. It was our Sunday special. An alternate meal was the stuffat tal-fenek, equally scrumptious!"

Ingredients

For the pastry:

pastry for 9-inch, double crust pie, recipe page 273
egg wash

For the filling:

1 cup whole-milk or part-skim ricotta
2 to 3 sprigs Italian parsley, minced
salt and white pepper
1 large egg, well beaten
1 can (12 ounces) corned beef, flaked
2 large potatoes, peeled and sliced
1 large onion, sliced
1 cup freshly shelled or frozen peas

Method

Preheat the oven to 375°F.

Place a freshly rolled out pie crust on a well-floured pie plate. With a fork, pierce the crust in several places. Pre-bake bottom pie crust for approximately 10 minutes. Ceramic or metal weights can be placed over wax or parchment paper to prevent pie crust from bubbling. Remove from oven and cool. Set aside.

In a large bowl, mix ricotta, parsley, salt and pepper to taste, and egg. Add flaked corned beef and mix well. Set aside.

Neatly layer sliced potatoes on the pastry crust. Add a layer of onions and follow with layers of peas, and the ricotta mixture. Cover filling with top pastry. Seal and flute edges. Brush top crust with egg wash. Create vent holes in top crust. Bake for approximately 45 minutes, or until crust becomes golden brown.

Serve piping hot.

3 to 4 servings.

Meat Pie 2

Torta tal-Laħam 2

This is the meat pie we eat in our home. Make two pies by doubling the quantities and freeze one for later use or make smaller, individual pies.

Ingredients

For the pastry:

pastry for a 9-inch double crust pie, recipe page 273
egg wash

For the filling:

1 large onion, peeled and chopped
1 to 2 cloves garlic, peeled and minced
2 tablespoons olive or other vegetable oil
1½ pounds lean beef, cut into one-inch cubes
2 large potatoes, peeled and sliced
3 large carrots, peeled, and sliced
1 large basil leaf, torn or 1 teaspoon dried basil, crushed
1 bay leaf
1 stalk celery
½ teaspoon curry powder
salt and freshly ground pepper
3 cans (15 ounces each) prepared tomato sauce
2 cups cold water
1 cup vegetable or chicken stock
1 cup freshly shelled or frozen peas

Method

Preheat the oven to 375°F.

Place a freshly rolled out pie crust on a well-floured pie plate. With a fork, pierce the crust in several places. Pre-bake bottom pie crust for approximately 10 to 15 minutes. Ceramic or metal weights can be placed over wax or parchment paper to prevent pie crust from bubbling. Remove from oven and cool. Set aside.

In large stockpot, sauté onion and garlic in olive oil until the onion becomes translucent, usually between 5 and 10 minutes. Add meat and sauté for approximately 15 minutes. Remove from heat. Drain off and discard excess fat. Add potatoes, carrots, basil, bay leaf, celery, curry powder, and salt and pepper to taste. Cover with tomato sauce, water, and stock. Simmer for approximately one hour, stirring occasionally, until vegetables are tender and the meat is cooked. Stir in peas in the last 10 minutes of cooking. Add more water if the stew appears to be drying out. Remove from heat. Remove bay leaf and celery stalk.

Carefully spoon stew into pre-baked pie shell. Cover filling with top pastry. Seal and flute edges. Brush top crust with egg wash. Create vent holes in top crust. Bake for approximately 45 minutes, or until crust becomes golden brown.

Serve piping hot.

3 to 4 servings.

Kitchen Notes

Most families prefer prepared Indian curry powders, not Jamaican curry powders for this stew. Other families substitute mixed spice for the curry powder or do not use either.

Stuffed Breast of Veal

Sidra tal-Vitella

Although veal is used infrequently in Malta except in distinctly Italian dishes, in the Caruana and Consiglio households in the United States, stuffed breast of veal is a Sunday favorite.

Ingredients

3 large potatoes, peeled and thinly sliced
4 to 6 tablespoons olive or other vegetable oil
1 breast of veal (approximately 3 to 4 pounds) with large pocket

For the stuffing:

½ cup unseasoned bread crumbs
½ pound lean ground beef or a combination of beef and pork
1 medium onion, peeled and minced
1 to 2 cloves garlic, peeled and minced
2 tablespoons unsalted butter or margarine, softened
1 to 2 sprigs Italian parsley, minced
1 sprig rosemary, crushed
2 sprigs fresh thyme, crushed
salt and freshly ground pepper

Method

Preheat the oven to 350°F.

Carefully line bottom of large casserole dish with the sliced potatoes. Sprinkle olive or other vegetable oil over the potatoes. Set aside.

For the filling:

In a large bowl, combine the stuffing ingredients. Set aside.

Making certain the veal breast pocket is open and pliable, carefully insert stuffing into cavity. Kitchen thread can be used to close the pocket, but usually is not necessary. Place veal on top of the layer of potatoes and roast for approximately 45 minutes to 1 hour, usually depending on the size of the breast of veal and the amount of stuffing. Meat stuffing must be well cooked. During cooking, turn potatoes over frequently and add water if the potatoes appear to be drying out.

If the potatoes are not cooked when the veal is done, put them back in the oven, covered with foil, for another 10 minutes.

Serve piping hot.

4 servings.

Kitchen Notes

Some families prefer not to use chopped meat for the stuffing. Increase the amount of bread crumbs if you do not use the meat, and add a small amount of water or a well-beaten egg to bind them.

Veal Olives

tal-Vitella Braġjoli

Alfred Grech likes to make brajjoli with veal cutlets. This is an adaption of his recipe.

Ingredients

1 large onion, peeled and chopped
1 to 2 cloves garlic, peeled and chopped
2 tablespoons olive or other vegetable oil
1 cup red wine
2 to 3 slices bacon, cooked, blotted, and chopped
4 hard-boiled eggs, shelled and cut into chunks
3 to 5 tablespoons bread crumbs (optional)
2 to 3 sprigs parsley, minced
salt and freshly ground pepper
4 thinly sliced and pounded veal cutlets

Method

In a large skillet, sauté onion and garlic in olive oil until onion is translucent, usually between 5 and 10 minutes. Add wine and reserve sauce. In small bowl, mix chopped bacon, hard-boiled eggs, bread crumbs, parsley, and salt and pepper. Set aside. Carefully place bacon and hard-boiled egg mixture in individual veal cutlets. Roll-up jelly-roll style, and tie securely with kitchen twine. Place in skillet and fry for approximately 15 minutes. Remove excess fat. Add sauce and simmer for approximately 20 more minutes, making certain the liquid does not dry up.

Serve piping hot.

3 to 4 servings.

Tripe Pie

Torta tal-Kirxa

Ingredients

For the pastry:

pastry for a 9-inch double crust pie, recipe page 273
egg wash

For the filling:

2 pounds tripe, cleaned, washed, and patted dried
2 large onions, peeled and chopped
1 to 2 cloves garlic, peeled and chopped
1 large tomato, peeled, seeded, and chopped
1 large eggplant, peeled and chopped
2 tablespoons tomato paste
¾ cup cold water
salt and freshly ground pepper

Method

Preheat the oven to 350°F.

Place a freshly rolled out pie crust on a well-floured pie plate. With a fork, pierce the crust in several places. Pre-bake bottom pie crust for approximately 10 to 15 minutes. Ceramic or metal weights can be placed over wax or parchment paper to prevent pie crust from bubbling. Remove from oven and cool. Set aside.

Cut tripe into pieces. Boil tripe tender, approximately one hour. Drain. Set aside. In a large skillet, sauté onions and garlic in olive oil until the onion becomes until translucent, usually between 8 to 10 minutes. Add tomato, eggplant, tomato paste, water, and salt and pepper to taste. Continue on low heat for approximately 30 minutes, making certain the mixture does not dry out. Remove from heat. Add tripe. Mix thoroughly. Set aside. Cool.

Carefully place tripe mixture into pre-baked pastry shell. Seal and flute edges. Brush with egg wash. Create vent holes in top crust. Bake for approximately 45 minutes, or until until crust is golden.

Serve piping hot.

3 to 4 servings.

Stuffed Chicken

Tiġieġa bil-Ħaxu

Ingredients

1 large roasting chicken (approximately 5 pounds) suitable for stuffing
1 large onion, peeled and sliced

For the stuffing:

½ cup unseasoned bread crumbs
1 slice cooked ham, shredded
1 to 2 sprigs Italian parsley, minced
1 sprig thyme, minced
1 sprig marjoram, minced
1 sage leaf, minced
½ stalk celery, chopped finely
1 tablespoon unsalted butter or margarine
1 hard-boiled egg, shelled and chopped (optional)
6 tablespoons water
salt and freshly ground pepper

Method

Preheat the oven to 350°F.

Carefully wash and rinse chicken. Pat dry with paper towel. Place chicken in a large, greased roasting pan. Place onion slices around the chicken. Heat in oven for approximately 45 minutes. Remove and cool.

In a large bowl, combine all stuffing ingredients. Set aside.

Carefully open cavity of the precooked chicken and add stuffing mixture. Cook for approximately 1 more hour or until the juices run clear.

Serve piping hot.

3 to 4 servings.

Kitchen Notes

Roast chicken is often served with roasted potatoes, which are layered beneath it on the roasting pan. Families concerned about the amount of chicken fat absorbed by the potatoes will usually make a separate dish of roasted potatoes (see recipe, page 131) and serve it with the chicken.

Stewed Pigeons

Beċċun Stuffat

Many of my Maltese friends would probably question my ethnic roots if I did not include at least one pigeon recipe in this collection. For readers who have not been to Malta please note: pigeons are specially raised for this very popular dish; these are not the pigeons North Americans see in the park or hovering around buildings! Friends visiting Gesters Restaurant in Xghra, Gozo rave about the pigeon stew and pigeon pie served there. If you want to try this dish in North America, contact one of the specialty provision mail-order companies listed in the resources section, or check with your local butcher. For the less adventuresome—like myself—rock cornish hens are an excellent substitute!

Ingredients

2 prepared squabs or 2 rock cornish hens

For the stuffing:

1 medium onion, peeled and chopped
1 to 2 cloves garlic, peeled and minced
2 tablespoons olive or other vegetable oil
½ pound lean ground beef or pork
1 cup unseasoned bread crumbs
1 teaspoon unsalted butter or margarine
2 to 3 sprigs Italian parsley, minced
1 egg, well beaten

For the sauce:

1 large onion, peeled and chopped
2 to 3 cloves garlic, peeled and minced
3 large, ripe tomatoes, chopped and seeded, or 1 can (28 ounces) peeled tomatoes can be substituted
1 to 2 sprigs fresh marjoram, chopped
1 to 2 small fresh or dried sage leaves, crushed
1 to 2 sprigs fresh thyme, chopped
salt and freshly ground pepper
5 cups cold water
3 cups chicken or vegetable stock

1 cup dry red wine

Method

Carefully rinse birds under running cold water. Pat dry. Set aside.

For the stuffing:

In a large skillet, sauté onion and garlic in olive oil until the onion becomes translucent, usually between 5 and 10 minutes. Add ground beef and gently simmer for 15 and 20 minutes, until meat becomes pink. Remove from heat. Drain off and discard excess fat. Set aside. Cool.

In a large bowl, combine bread crumbs with butter and parsley. Add cooked meat mixture and egg. Mix well. Insert stuffing inside birds' cavity and sew closed with kitchen thread. Place birds in stockpot of boiling water for approximately 25 minutes. Remove birds from water. Set aside.

For the sauce:

In a large skillet, sauté onion and garlic in olive oil until the onion becomes translucent, usually between 5 and 10 minutes. Add tomatoes, marjoram, sage, thyme, and salt and pepper to taste. Cover with water and stock, bring to a boil, and simmer for approximately 10 to 15 minutes. Transfer sauce to large stockpot. Add birds and the wine and simmer for approximately 25 minutes, or until cooked.

Serve with spaghetti and vegetables.

3 to 4 servings.

Kitchen Notes

Many traditional recipes for stewed pigeon call for stuffing the bird with uncooked chopped meat. Due to concerns about salmonella in North America, this practice is not recommended here.

Pigeon Pie

Torta tal-Beċċun

Ingredients

For the pastry:

pastry for a 9-inch double crust pie, recipe page 273
egg wash

For the filling:

2 large onions, peeled and chopped
1 to 2 cloves garlic, minced
2 tablespoons olive or other vegetable oil
3 prepared swabs or rock cornish hens, well rinsed and patted dry
1 large leek, cleaned and sliced
2 carrots, peeled and diced
2 to 3 large potatoes, peeled and diced
2 to 3 large ripe tomatoes or 1 can (28 ounces) peeled or crushed tomatoes
2 teaspoons tomato paste
2 to 3 sprigs, Italian parsley, minced
1 bay leaf
1 to 2 sprigs fresh mint, minced
salt and freshly ground pepper
2 cups cold water
2 cups vegetable or chicken stock

Method

Preheat the oven to 350° F.

Place a freshly rolled out pie crust on a well-floured pie plate. With a fork, pierce the crust in several places. Pre-bake bottom pie crust for approximately 10 minutes. Ceramic or metal weights can be placed over wax or parchment paper to prevent pie crust from bubbling. Remove from oven and cool. Set aside.

In a large skillet, sauté onion and garlic in olive oil until the onion becomes translucent, usually between 5 and 10 minutes. Add the birds, leeks, carrots, potatoes, tomatoes, tomato paste, parsley, bay leaf, mint, and salt and pepper to taste. Cover with water and stock.

Simmer for approximately 30 minutes or until the meat begins to fall off the bones of the birds. Remove from heat.

Carefully remove and discard all bones from the birds and return the meat to the mixture. Remove and discard bay leaf. Spoon bird and vegetable mixture in precooked pastry-lined plate. Cover filling with top pastry. Seal and flute edges. Brush top crust with egg wash. Create vent holes in top crust. Bake for approximately 45 minutes, or until the crust becomes golden brown.

Serve piping hot.

3 to 4 servings.

Variations

Instead of cooking the potatoes with the birds and other vegetables, some Maltese families will cook the potatoes separately and then mash them. The mashed potatoes then are spread on the precooked bottom crust. The bird and vegetable mixture is carefully layered on top of the potatoes. The filling is covered with top pastry and sealed (see instructions above) before cooking.

Chapter 9

Desserts

Diżerta

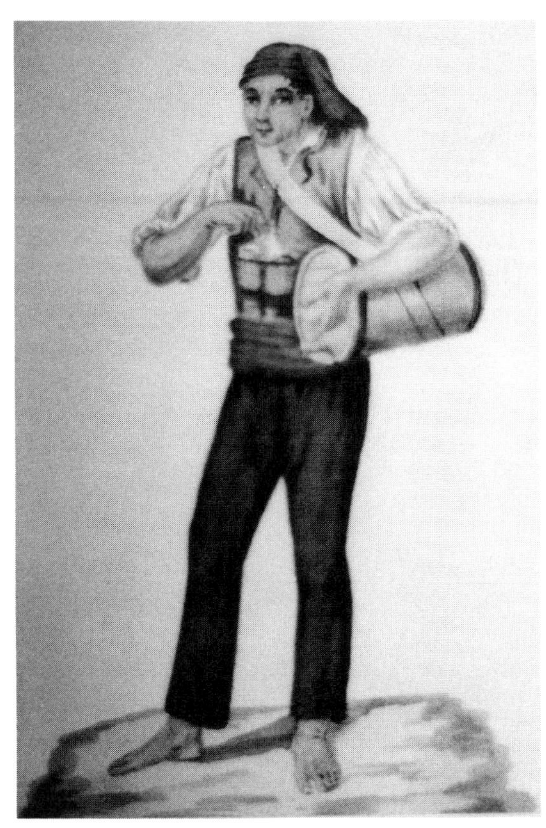

Cocoa-Date Pie

Torta tat-Tamal u Cocoa

This recipe is adapted from Louisette San Manduca, owner of Fontanella's Tea House, Mdina, Malta.

Ingredients

For the pastry:

pastry for a 9-inch double pie crust, see recipe page 273

For the filling:

1 pound dates, pitted and chopped
½ cup milk
½ cup cold water
½ cup unsweetened cocoa
1 cup orange juice
shot glass Sambuca or other anise liqueur
2 ounces walnuts, chopped
zest of orange rind
¼ cup granulated sugar
2 eggs, beaten

Method

Preheat oven to 350°F.

Soak the pitted dates in milk and water for approximately 20 minutes. Set aside.

Place a freshly rolled out pie crust on a well-floured pie plate. With a fork, pierce the crust in several places. Pre-bake bottom pie crust for approximately 10 minutes. Ceramic or metal weights can be placed over wax or parchment paper to prevent pie crust from bubbling. Remove from oven and cool. Set aside.

Simmer over low heat the cocoa, orange juice, Sambuca, walnuts, orange rind, and sugar for ½ hour. Add chopped dates and well-beaten eggs to the mixture. Stir well.

Carefully spoon mixture into pre-baked pie crust. Cover pie with top crust. Seal and flute edge. Cut several vent holes to permit steam to escape. Bake for approximately 45 minutes, or until crust becomes golden brown.

Best served cold.

5 to 6 servings.

Sweet Ricotta Pie

Ħelwa ta' l-Irkotta

Ingredients

For the pastry:

pastry for a 9-inch double crust pie, see page 273

egg wash

For the filling:

2 pounds whole-milk or part-skim ricotta

2 tablespoons confectioners' sugar

1 egg, well beaten

2 heaping tablespoons unsweetened cocoa, or 2 ounces unsweetened chocolate, slivered

1 teaspoon pure vanilla extract

Method

Preheat the oven to 375°F.

Place a freshly rolled out pie crust on a well-floured pie plate. With a fork, pierce the crust in several places. Pre-bake bottom pie crust for approximately 10 minutes. Ceramic or metal weights can be placed over wax or parchment paper to prevent pie crust from bubbling. Remove from oven and cool. Set aside.

In a large bowl, mix ricotta, sugar, and egg until smooth with a hand beater. Add cocoa and vanilla and blend again. Spoon filling into the precooked pie crust. Roll out remaining pastry for top crust and cut into lattice strips with a pastry wheel. Layer the strips over the pie in a criss-cross fashion. With a pastry brush, brush egg wash on lattice strips. Bake for approximately 30 to 45 minutes, or until lattice turns golden brown.

Serve either hot or cold.

4 to 6 servings.

Unsweetened Ricotta Pie

Torta ta' l-Irkotta

Ingredients

For the pastry:

pastry for a 9-inch double crust pie, see page 273
egg wash

For the filling:

2 pounds whole-milk or part-skim ricotta
2 eggs, well beaten
4 sprigs Italian parsley, minced
salt and freshly ground pepper

Method

Preheat the oven to 375°F.

Place a freshly rolled out pie crust on a well-floured pie plate. With a fork, pierce the crust in several places. Pre-bake bottom pie crust for approximately 10 minutes. Ceramic or metal weights can be placed over wax or parchment paper to prevent pie crust from bubbling. Remove from oven and cool. Set aside.

In a large bowl, mix ricotta and eggs with a hand beater until smooth. Add parsley, and salt and pepper to taste, and mix again. Carefully spoon mixture into the pre-baked pie crust. Roll out remaining pastry for top crust and cut into lattice strips with a pastry wheel. Layer the strips in a criss-cross fashion over the pie. With a pastry brush, brush egg wash on lattice strips. Bake for approximately 30 to 45 minutes, or until the lattice turns golden brown.

Serve either warm or cold.

4 to 6 servings.

Variations

In the spring when fava beans are small, many Maltese families will include a handful of them with the ricotta mixture.

Kitchen Notes

Although this pie is served as a dessert, it can also be an entree served with side dishes of vegetables or salad in some Maltese homes.

Fried Date Slices

Imqaret

Ingredients

For the pastry:

1 tablespoon vegetable shortening or lard
1 tablespoon unsalted butter or margarine
1 cup all-purpose unbleached flour, sifted
1 tablespoon sugar
1 teaspoon anisette liqueur
1 to 2 teaspoons orange flower water

For the filling:

1 pound dates, pitted and chopped
milk or water for soaking dates
1 teaspoon cloves
zest of 1 lemon or orange
1 shot glass of anise liqueur
1 tablespoon orange flower water
sufficient vegetable oil for deep frying

Method

For the pastry: Cut in the shortening and butter into the flour with a pastry blender. Add sugar, anisette, and orange flower water. Form pastry into a ball. Wrap in tea cloth or plastic wrap and refrigerate for approximately one hour.

For the filling: Soak the dates in a small amount of milk or water for approximately 30 minutes. Add cloves, lemon zest, anise liqueur, and flower water. Mix well. Set aside.

On well-floured pastry board or other hard surface, roll out dough into a long, wide strip. Spread date mixture in the middle of the strip. Fold pastry over and seal carefully. Cut sealed strip into "diamond" shapes. Press edges of individual "diamonds" closed. Fry in heated deep oil until crisp and golden brown. Remove from oil and drain on absorbent paper.

Serve hot.

3 to 4 servings.

Almond and Chocolate Pie

Torta tal-Marmurat

Ingredients

For the pastry:

2 cups all-purpose, unbleached flour, sifted
1 teaspoon sugar
1 tablespoons unsweetened cocoa
2 tablespoons unsalted butter or margarine
2 tablespoons vegetable shortening or lard
¼ to ½ cup ice water
egg wash

For the filling:

1 cup freshly shelled almonds, ground
½ cup confectioners' sugar
2 tablespoons unsweetened cocoa
1 teaspoon mixed spice
1 teaspoon nutmeg
zest of one lemon
2 eggs, well beaten

Method

Preheat the oven to 375°F.

For the pastry: In a large bowl sift together flour, sugar, and cocoa. With a pastry blender, cut in unsalted butter and shortening. Add ice water, make into dough, and form into a ball. Cover tightly with a tea cloth or plastic wrap. Refrigerate for at least one hour before rolling out.

For the filling: In a large bowl, mix ground almonds with the sugar. Add cocoa, mixed spice, nutmeg, and lemon zest. Fold in beaten eggs and mix well. Set aside.

On well-floured pastry board or other hard surface, roll out dough, making certain to roll out only in one direction. Line pie plate with pastry dough and bake in oven for approximately 10 minutes. Remove and cool. Spoon almond mixture into cooled pastry shell. Roll out remaining pastry and cut into lattice strips. Arrange strips on pie in a criss-cross fashion. With a pastry brush, brush egg wash on lattice. Bake for approximately 30 to 45 minutes, or until the lattice becomes golden brown.

Serve either hot or cold.

4 to 6 servings.

Almond Macaroons

Biskuttini tal-Lewż

Ingredients

¾ cup brown sugar
¾ cup freshly shelled almonds, ground
½ cup rice flour
2 eggs, well beaten
1 teaspoon pure vanilla extract
slivered almond slices for garnish

Method

Preheat the oven to 400°F.

In a large bowl, mix sugar, almonds, and rice flour with a hand or electric beater. Fold in the well-beaten eggs. Add vanilla extract and blend well. Form dough into a ball. Cover tightly with a tea cloth or plastic wrap. Refrigerate for at least one hour.

Carefully drop tablespoons of the dough on a cookie sheet lined with parchment or rice paper. Bake for approximately 10 minutes or until drops are well set. Garnish with slivered almond slices. Cool on cookie rack.

Serve either hot or cold.

Makes approximately 10 quarter-size cookies

Chestnut Pie

Torta tal-Qastan

Ingredients

For the tart shell pastry:

pastry for a 9-inch double crust pie, see page 273
egg wash

For the filling:

1 pound chestnuts, soaked overnight and peeled or boiled in water for approximately 15 minutes until shells can be removed easily
1/3 cup golden raisins (sultanas) (optional)
2 heaping tablespoons unsweetened cocoa
1 grated orange or tangerine rind
sugar to taste (usually ½ cup)
dash mixed spice or cinnamon and cloves

Method

Preheat the oven to 375°F.

Place a freshly rolled out pie crust on a well-floured pie plate. With a fork, pierce the crust in several places. Pre-bake bottom pie crust for approximately 10 minutes. Ceramic or metal weights can be placed over wax or parchment paper to prevent pie crust from bubbling. Remove from oven and cool. Set aside.

In medium size saucepot, place chestnuts and raisins in a small amount of water. Bring to a boil and then reduce heat. Add cocoa, orange rind, sugar, and mixed spice. Simmer and stir for 5 to 10 minutes. Remove from heat.

In a food processor or blender, grind chestnut mixture on pulse speed until smooth.

Carefully spoon chestnut mixture into the pre-baked pie shell. Cover filling with top pastry. Seal and flute edges. Brush top crust with egg wash. Create vent holes in top crust. Bake for approximately 45 minutes, or until the crust becomes golden brown.

Serve either hot or cold.

3 to 4 servings.

Variations

Some families prefer to make tartlettes with this filling instead.

Chestnut and Date Pie

Torta tal-Imqaret u l-Qastan

Ingredients

For the pastry:

pastry for a 9-inch double crust pie, see page 273
egg wash

For the filling:

1 cup pitted cherries (reserve liquid)
½ pound chestnuts, soaked overnight and peeled or boiled in water until the shells can be easily removed
½ pound dates, pitted, chopped, soaked in orange juice for ½ hour
1 egg, well beaten
½ teaspoon mixed spice
zest from one orange

Method

Preheat the oven to 375°F.

Place a freshly rolled out pie crust on a well-floured pie plate. With a fork, pierce the crust in several places. Pre-bake bottom pie crust for approximately 10 minutes. Ceramic or metal weights can be placed over wax or parchment paper to prevent pie crust from bubbling. Remove from oven and cool. Set aside.

In food processor or blender, grind cherries and cooked chestnuts on pulse speed. Remove from processor. Spoon in chopped dates, egg, mixed spice, and orange zest. Make certain the mixture is smooth.

Carefully spoon mixture into pre-baked pie shell. Cover filling with top pastry. Seal and flute edges. Brush top crust with egg wash. Create vent holes in top crust. Bake for approximately 45 minutes, or until crust becomes golden brown.

Serve either hot or cold.

4 to 5 servings.

Ricotta and Almond Pie

Torta ta' l-Irkotta u Lewż

Ingredients

For the pastry:

pastry for a 9-inch double crust pie, see page 273
egg wash

For the filling:

1 cup whole-milk or part-skim ricotta
1 cup freshly shelled almonds, ground
½ cup confectioners' sugar
2 eggs, well beaten
1 cup pitted sour cherries, rinsed and well drained

Method

Preheat the oven to 375°F.

Place a freshly rolled out pie crust on a well-floured pie plate. With a fork, pierce the crust in several places. Pre-bake bottom pie crust for approximately 10 minutes. Ceramic or metal weights can be placed over wax or parchment paper to prevent pie crust from bubbling. Remove from oven and cool. Set aside.

Pulse in a food processor or use an electric beater to blend ricotta, almonds, sugar, and eggs. Add cherries and mix. Carefully spoon ricotta mixture into a pre-baked pie shell. Cover with top pastry. Seal and flute edges. Brush pastry with egg wash. Create vent holes in top crust. Bake for approximately 30 to 45 minutes, or until the crust becomes golden brown.

Serve either hot or cold.

3 to 4 servings.

Bread Pudding

Pudina tal-Ħobż

Wilfred Camilleri provided this recipe.

Ingredients

1½ pounds stale bread
2 cups milk
1 tablespoon unsalted butter or margarine
3½ ounces granulated sugar
2 ounces candied fruit, chopped
2 tablespoons unsweetened cocoa powder
shot glass of brandy or rum
2 eggs, well-beaten
1 teaspoon pure vanilla extract
½ cup raisins, soaked in orange juice
grated peel from one orange
¼ cup freshly shelled almonds, crushed

Method

Preheat the oven to 350°F.

Remove all bread crusts. Soak the bread in the milk until it becomes soft. Add the butter, sugar, candied fruit, cocoa powder, and brandy to the bread and milk mixture. Mix well. Fold in beaten eggs. Add vanilla extract, raisins, and orange peel, and mix thoroughly again. Place mixture in a well greased and floured baking dish.

Sprinkle the crushed almonds on top of the mixture and bake for approximately 30 to 45 minutes, or until an inserted cake tester comes clean.

Serve cold.

3 to 4 servings.

Ricotta Cannoli

Kannoli ta'l-Irkotta

Although in days past, many Maltese cooks made the cannoli shells themselves, store-bought shells work well for this easy-to-prepare make-ahead crowd pleaser. There are several in my freezer now!

Ingredients

1½ pounds whole-milk or part-skim ricotta
4 tablespoons confectioners' sugar
3 ounces dark chocolate, grated or 3 tablespoons unsweetened cocoa
3 ounces candied lemon peel or candied cherries
2 ounces freshly shelled almonds, ground (optional)
6 pre-made, packaged cannoli shells (available in Italian groceries or specialty stores)

Method

In a large bowl, combine ricotta, sugar, and chocolate with a hand mixer. Add candied peel and ground almonds. Using either a small dessert spoon or pastry tube, carefully fill each cannoli shell. Refrigerate before serving.

Serve with coffee.

Makes 6 cannoli

Kitchen Notes

Wrap *Kannoli* in freezer paper or air tight plastic bags before storing in the freezer. Let thaw at room temperature for approximately 20 minutes before serving.

Date Roll

Pasta tat-Tamal

Ingredients

For the pastry:

1½ cups all-purpose unbleached flour, sifted
3 ounces granulated sugar
1 cup (2 sticks) unsalted butter or margarine

For the filling:

8 ounces pitted dates, chopped finely and soaked in orange juice for approximately ½ hour
2 tablespoons unsalted butter or margarine
1 shot glass anisette liqueur or 1 teaspoon anisette extract

Method

Preheat the oven to 350°F.

For the pastry:

In a large bowl, sift flour and sugar. Cut in unsalted butter or margarine with a pastry blender. Add water as necessary to bind. Wrap in plastic wrap and refrigerate for at least one hour.

For the filling:

In a large bowl mix dates with the butter and anisette. Transfer to a small saucepot and simmer over low heat, stirring ingredients until they are smooth. Cool and set aside.

Roll out dough into an oblong shape. Spread cooled mixture evenly on the pastry. Roll up, jelly-roll style, and flute edges to seal. Bake for approximately 1 hour on a well-greased cookie sheet. Thoroughly cool and then slice.

5 to 6 servings.

Village Biscuits

Buskuttini tar-Raħal

Ingredients

1 cup all-purpose unbleached flour, sifted
1 cup granulated sugar
2 ounces unsalted butter or margarine
grated peel from small lemon
grated peel from small orange
½ teaspoon ground cloves
1 teaspoon unsweetened cocoa powder
1 egg, slightly beaten
2 ounces milk
confectioners' sugar for dusting

Method

Preheat the oven to 350°F.

In a large bowl, mix together flour and sugar. With a pastry blender, cut in butter or margarine until the mixture resembles a fine cornmeal. Add the lemon peel, orange peel, cloves, and cocoa and blend well. Add beaten egg and milk. Form the dough into elongated biscuits, flatten slightly and place on a well-greased and floured baking sheet. Sprinkle fine sugar on top of each biscuit. Bake for approximately 20 minutes until golden. Cool on wire rack.

Serve at room temperature.

Makes approximately 10 biscuits.

Christening Biscuits

Biskuttini tal-Magħmudija

Although these biscuits traditionally were served when a baby was baptized, you'll see them served at other family events.

Ingredients

8 eggs, separated
1 cup granulated sugar
1 cup brown sugar
½ teaspoon cinnamon
½ teaspoon ground cloves
4 ounces candied lemon or citron peel
½ teaspoon anise extract
1 teaspoon baking soda
2 cups all-purpose unbleached flour, sifted
pastel colored icing for decorating

Method

Preheat the oven to 400°F.

Using an electric or hand beater, beat the egg whites until stiff. Gradually add egg yolks and sugars, cinnamon, cloves, peel, anise, and baking soda. Stir in the flour, making certain the mixture is smooth. Set aside. Form into two balls. Wrap in plastic wrap or cover with a tea cloth and refrigerate for one hour.

Place parchment or rice paper on large cookie sheet. Sprinkle flour on the paper. Drop teaspoon-size amounts of the dough on the parchment paper. Bake for approximately 15 to 20 minutes, or until the biscuits turn golden brown. Cool. Carefully remove from parchment paper. Drizzle pastel icing on each biscuit.

Serve with coffee or tea.

Makes approximately one dozen biscuits.

Sesame Rings 1

Qagħaq tal-Ġulġlien 1

Michael Zarb remembers these rings, sometimes referred to as 'kaghak tal-hlewwa' (or qaghaq tal-hlewwa), as bagel-size dough rings made of flour, yeast, sugar, anise seed, and grated orange and lemon peel. "Mother used to get this dough from the baker. The dough rings were sprinkled with sesame seed and left to rise on spread bran, to prevent sticking. I suppose this also added to their peculiarity. They were then baked in the baker's oven. My siblings and I used to sell the 'kaghak' knocking door-to-door, one of our few sources of income in the thirties. At times, there were disasters—if the baker did not put them in the oven before they rose. Then, they would go flat and hard, surely unsellable, and became the family food."

This recipe was provided by Sandro Grima.

Ingredients

1 cup bottled water heated to 120°F
½ cup sugar
1½ packets active dry yeast
1 cup all-purpose unbleached flour (enough to turn the 1 cup of water to a soft dough)
¼ teaspoon orange extract
1/8 teaspoon lemon extract
1/8 teaspoon anise extract
1 teaspoon freshly grated orange zest
1 teaspoon caraway seeds
1 stick melted sweet butter or margarine
½ teaspoon salt
sesame seeds for sprinkling
3 to 4 ice cubes
butter

Method

Preheat oven to 375°F.

In a large bowl, mix water, 1 tablespoon sugar, yeast, and 2 tablespoons of flour. Wait until very frothy, about 15 minutes. Add orange extract, lemon extract, anise extract, orange zest, caraway seeds, butter, and salt. Start adding remaining flour 1 cup at a time until you form a soft dough. Let dough rest for 15 minutes and then knead well. Let dough rest for 15 minutes and then knead for a few minutes. Place dough in a large bowl and cover with plastic wrap.

Let dough stand in a warm place (80°F to 85°F) until it doubles. Knead dough lightly and form into rings. These rings will rise substantially, so you need to start with a diameter slightly thicker than a pencil. Sprinkle lightly with sesame seeds. Let stand on a non-stick cookie sheet in a warm place until they double—or even better triple—in volume.

Place cookie sheet with rings in the oven. Before you close it, place 3 to 4 ice cubes in the oven bottom to create moisture as they melt. Lower temperature to 350°F. Cook until the tops start turning golden. Remove from oven. Glaze the tops with melted butter and cook until brown.

Serve hot.

Makes approximately 18 rings.

Sesame Rings 2

Qagħaq tal-Ġulġlien 2

This is an easier, non-yeast version of Qaghaq tal-Gulglien, which is quite good.

Ingredients

4 cups all-purpose unbleached flour, sifted
2 teaspoons baking powder
½ teaspoon salt
½ to ¾ cup granulated sugar
4 ounces vegetable shortening (lard frequently is used)
4 ounces butter or margarine
2 eggs, well beaten
1 teaspoon anise extract or anise liquer
zest from orange and lemon or 1 teaspoon orange extract and 1 teaspoon lemon extract
½ cup milk or water
sesame seeds for sprinkling

Method

Preheat the oven to 375°F.

In a large bowl, sift together flour, baking powder, and salt. Set aside. With an electric mixer or hand-head beater, mix sugar, shortening, and butter. Stir in eggs. Slowly add anise extract, orange zest, lemon zest, and milk to make a dough. Form dough into small rings and place on a cookie tray lined with parchment or rice paper. Sprinkle sesame seeds over each ring. Bake for approximately 30 minutes, or until the rings turn golden. Check for doneness with a cake tester or tooth pick.

Serve hot.

Makes approximately six, bagel-size rings.

Hard Crackers

Galletti

Ingredients

1 teaspoon salt
2 cups all-purpose, unbleached flour, sifted
2 cups semolina
1 ounce fresh yeast or 2 packets dried yeast
2 cups warm bottled water (approximately 120°F)

Method

Preheat the oven at 450°F.

In a large bowl, sift together salt and flour. Sift in the semolina. Set aside. Dissolve the yeast in a little water; add to the dry ingredients. Slowly add the remaining water and mix. Knead for approximately five minutes, until smooth. Cover bowl with a damp cloth, place in a warm location, and allow to double in size, approximately one hour. Divide into four balls and roll out each as thinly as possible on a well-floured marble or hard surface. Use a 2-inch diameter biscuit or pastry cutter to form the crackers. Transfer each cracker onto a well-greased and floured baking tray. With a fork, prick each biscuit. Bake until crispy and golden brown, approximately 10 to 15 minutes.

Serve with appetizers or cheese.

Makes approximately 15 biscuits.

Kitchen Notes

Expect these crackers to be "bumpy-looking." In Malta, two sizes of galletti usually are available, large, and small. Both are used with hors d'oeuvres.

Pomegranates with Orange Flower Water

Rummien fl-Ilma Żahar

When my nieces were young, they always wondered what people would want to do with all those "nasty seeds" in pomegranates. This is a simple and often overlooked recipe, that makes tasty use of those "nasty" seeds. Pomegranate trees grow in many Maltese home gardens.

Ingredients

seeds from 4 ripe pomegranates
1 tablespoon lemon juice
1 teaspoon orange flower water

Method

In medium size bowl, gently toss pomegranate seeds in the lemon juice and orange flower water. Place mixture in four individual dessert dishes and refrigerate. Serve chilled.

4 servings.

Kitchen Notes

This makes for a refreshing dessert in North American homes in late fall and early winter when summer's bounty of fruit is many months away.

Baked Stuffed Oranges

Larinġ Mimli l-Forn

This unusual recipe is especially popular when blood oranges are available in the winter.

Ingredients

4 large oranges, peeled and sectioned
5 to 6 pitted dates, chopped and soaked in orange juice or milk for 30 minutes to soften
1 to 2 ounces freshly shelled almonds, crushed
2 to 3 tablespoons honey
squeeze of lemon
2 cups hot water

Method

Preheat oven to 350°F.

Place the peeled and sectioned oranges close together in small casserole dish. Set aside.

In a small bowl, combine dates and almonds. Carefully spoon the mixture inside the sectioned oranges. Set aside. Pour hot water on the bottom of a casserole dish. Carefully place orange in casserole dish. Drizzle honey and the squeeze of lemon over the dates and almonds. Bake for approximately 15 minutes. Remove from heat. Serve chilled.

4 servings.

Almond and Fruit Sherbet

Ruġġata tal-Lewż

Although this is often referred to as a sherbert, it is actually served as a drink. Several older friends fondly remember sipping ruggata tal-lewz on hot, humid afternoons in Malta.

Ingredients

6 cups cold bottled water
1½ cups granulated sugar
1 teaspoon cinnamon
8 cloves
peel from one lemon
1 teaspoon almond extract
1 teaspoon pure vanilla extract
milk
ice cubes

Method

In large saucepot, bring to a boil water, sugar, cinnamon, cloves, and lemon peel, for approximately 20 minutes. Remove from heat. Cool. Using cheesecloth or fine gauge strainer, carefully strain mixture. Discard peel and cloves. Add almond and vanilla extracts to the liquid. Stir well. Pour in 2 bottles, cap, and store in refrigerator until ready to use.

For use: When ready to make sherbert-drinks, add four ounces of almond mixture to every four ounces of milk. Stir in ice cubes. Sip and relax.

Makes approximately eight, 8-ounce drinks.

Feasts and Sweets

Although fresh fruit usually is a welcome dessert, the Maltese have a passion for sweets, many of which are seasonal or linked with religious holidays such as Christmas and Easter or patron saint festivals or *festas.*

Today, there are no less than 150 extravagant village or town *festas,* usually held on weekends from February through December on both Malta and Gozo. Originally, *festas* were small, local celebrations honoring a patron saint, with a generous nobleman providing food and wine. When the Knights ruled Malta, they paid for the festivities, which became more elaborate. With British rule, new dimensions were added, such as music from brass bands. Individual parishes began picking up the tab, and rivalries grew among the bands and the villagers as to which would have the best *festa.*

Preparations for *festas* take months to complete. Typically, streets are decorated with flags, streamers, pendants, and lights. *Festas* begin with a religious service at church followed by a procession. Soon after, the sky lights up with noisy and colorful fireworks displays called *giggifogu,* similar to the Italian term, *guoco di fuoco.* Brass bands play into the early morning hours. Food stands are everywhere. Very visible are stands selling *Qubbajt,* nougat. There are two types of this nougat—one hard, made with almonds and sesame seeds, and the other soft, containing candied fruit peels. Both are similar to the nougat popular in Middle Eastern countries.

Family visits are *de rigueur* during *festas,* and you're expected to peek into the homes of Maltese families who deliberately leave their front doors open for this purpose during the festivities.

Carnival, held before the beginning of Lent in Valletta, is similar to Mardi Gras celebrations, with many paraders dressed in colorful costumes. *Prinjolata,* a traditional carnival sweet — actually an elaborate, iced sponge cake decorated with nuts and candied peel that most families purchase at confectionery stores, rather than make themselves— is available everywhere.

Kwarezimal, Lenten biscuits made with ground almonds and brown sugar with crushed almonds sprinkled on top, are made without eggs or fats in deference to ancient religious dictates about sacrifice during the season.

The Wednesday before Holy Week begins, many churches have Last Supper displays — tables set for Christ and his 12 apostles — with a variety of traditional foods and pastries.

Hard candy, traditionally sold on Good Friday, is made from syrup extracted from the dried pulp of carob. The syrup, *gulepp tal-harrub*, usually diluted with warm water, is a well-known cough and cold remedy available in Maltese pharmacies.

Easter is a family feast with relatives bringing a *figolla* — pastry cut into identical shapes such as lambs, or little girls, and filled with marzipan. The top has a pastel icing and a small, colored chocolate egg wrapped in colored foil is inserted at its center.

According to mythology, Phoenicians offered eggs to the fertility goddess Astarte. Both the ancient Egyptians and Persians gave eggs as gifts at the beginning of Spring. The Romans had figurines of young women decorated with fruit and eggs.

Figolla comes from the Sicilian word, *figurella*. It is believed that breadsellers in the past decided to sweeten unleavened bread, *il-ftira*, and put a decorated egg on it. Usually, the egg was colored red, as a symbol of prosperity. Chocolate or pastel colored eggs are used today.

While *Xkunvat* (pastry ribbons), made from flour, orange flower water, anisette, and drizzled with honey are traditionally served on St. John's day, June 24th — a feast dating to the Knights — they frequently are made for birthdays.

A filling nut cake is traditionally served on St. Martin's Day, celebrated November 10.

During the Christmas season, look for *Qaghaq ta-Kavatelli*, a rich almond and honey dessert, and *imbuljuta*, a hot chestnut and cocoa soup, which traditionally is served on Christmas Eve. *Qaghaq tal-ghasel*, honey rings, and *torta-tal marmurata*, almond pie, usually available year round, were once made only at Christmas.

At special occasions, *Biskuttini tal-lewz*, almond macaroons, and *Biskuttini tal-Maghmudija*, christening biscuits flavored with anise, are served.

You'll always find *kannoli ta' l-irkotta*, made with ricotta and similar to Italian cannoli, and *imqaret*, fried date cakes flavored with anise, orange, and tangerine, in pastry shops year-round. *Imqaret* also are popular in food stands during *festas*.

Lenten Sweet

Kwareżimal

Pronounced KWAREZEEMAL or KUARAIZEEMAL, the word refers to lenten sermons or baked marzipan. There are several accounts of why Kwarezimal, sweet by most accounts, were allowed during Lent. Early recipes, and there are many variations, used no fats in their preparation, since fats in earlier days may have been animal-based; refraining from meat was required during Lent. We know, today, what our ancestors may not have known — there is fat in those almonds!

Ingredients

3 ounces, freshly shelled almonds, ground
3 ounces all-purpose, unbleached flour, sifted
3 ounces rice flour
4 ½ ounces brown sugar
a pinch of ground cloves
½ teaspoon mixed spice
1 tablespoon unsweetened cocoa
1 orange rind, grated
1 lemon rind, grated
1 teaspoon orange flower water
1 teaspoon pure vanilla extract
water to bind
honey
3 tablespoons slivered almonds

Method

Preheat the oven to 375°F.

Mix the first 9 ingredients together. Add orange flower water, vanilla, and enough water to form a stiff dough. Refrigerate for approximately 1 hour. Cut dough into ten 3-inch long bars and flatten. Place in a well-greased baking pan. Flatten each piece with the back of a spoon. Bake for approximately 20 minutes, until the bars turn golden. Remove from oven. While still hot, drizzle with honey and top with slivered almonds.

Makes approximately 10 bars.

Easter Specialty

Figolli

Although this traditional Maltese treat is seen in pastry store windows in the weeks before Easter, many Maltese home cooks still take the time to make them. This recipe is adapted from Rita Camilleri, who lives outside of Toronto.

Ingredients

For the pastry:

½ cup shortening (part unsalted butter or margarine)
1 cup granulated sugar
1 egg, slightly beaten
1 teaspoon pure vanilla extract
2 cups all-purpose unbleached flour
1 teaspoon baking powder
½ teaspoon baking soda
½ teaspoon salt
1 cup sour cream or plain low-fat yogurt

For the almond paste:

1 cup freshly shelled almonds, grated
½ cup confectioners' sugar
½ cup granulated sugar
2 eggs, well beaten
1 teaspoon pure almond extract
1 teaspoon sugar syrup (such as Lyles golden syrup or Karo syrup)
sherry (to taste)

colored icing (optional)
hollow chocolate eggs (optional)

Method

For the pastry:

In a large bowl, mix shortening, sugar, egg and vanilla extract thoroughly. Sift together the flour, baking powder, baking soda, and salt. Add flour mixture to sugar mixture, alternating with sour cream.

Mix well to form dough. Divide dough and wrap tightly in plastic wrap. Refrigerate for at least one hour.

For the almond paste:

In a large bowl, mix the almonds with confectioners' sugar and granulated sugar. Beat the eggs with the almond extract, syrup, and sherry. Combine the egg mixture with the almond mixture until smooth. Set aside.

Putting the Figolli together:

Preheat the oven to 375°F.

On a well-floured, hard surface, roll out dough until it is approximately 1 inch thick. Cut into desired shapes (two cut-outs for each Figolla). Spread almond paste on one of the cut-outs. Place the other cut-out on top and press the edges to seal. Brush the top of the Figolli with the beaten egg. Bake until the Figolli turns golden. Let the Figolli cool and then decorate with colored icing. Place a hollow chocolate egg in the center of each Figolla using some soft icing to hold it in place.

Makes 1 large Figolla or several smaller Figolli, depending on cut-out size.

Pastry Ribbons

Xkunvat

Although these originally were made for the feast of St. John in June, many Maltese parents make them for their children's birthdays. Of course, you don't need a party to serve them!

Ingredients

2 cups all-purpose unbleached flour, sifted
2 tablespoons sugar
2 tablespoons unsalted butter or margarine
2 egg yolks, beaten
1 shot glass anisette liqueur or 1 teaspoon anisette extract
sufficient vegetable oil for deep frying
honey
sprinkles (optional)

Method

In a large bowl, sift flour and sugar. With a pastry blender, cut in unsalted butter or margarine. Add egg yolks and anisette. Mix well and form into a ball. Cover with tea cloth or plastic wrap and refrigerate for at least two hours.

On well-floured pastry board or other hard surface, roll out dough as thinly as possible. Cut into long strips and curl into knots. Fry in heated deep oil until crisp and golden. Remove from oil and drain on absorbent paper. While ribbons are still hot, pour honey on each strip and decorate with sprinkles.

Serve hot.

Makes approximately 10 ribbons.

Vittorin Sweet

Helwa tal-Vittorin

The Feast of Il-Vittorja (Our Lady of Victories) is celebrated September 8th commemerating both the exit of the Turks in 1565 after the Great Siege and the birth of the Virgin Mary.

Ingredients

For the pastry:

pastry for a 9-inch double crust pie, see page 273
egg wash

For the filling:

1 cup cherry pie filling, jam, or fruit preserves
grated rind from one large lemon
juice of one large lemon
½ teaspoon pure almond extract
1 cup unseasoned bread crumbs

Method

Preheat the oven to 375°F.

Place a freshly rolled out pie crust on a well-floured pie plate. With a fork, pierce the crust in several places. Pre-bake bottom pie crust for approximately 10 minutes. Ceramic or metal weights can be placed over wax or parchment paper to prevent pie crust from bubbling. Remove from oven and cool. Set aside.

In large bowl, mix filling with grated lemon rind, lemon juice, and almond extract. Add bread crumbs. Mix well.

Carefully spoon jam and bread crumb mixture in pre-baked pie crust. With remaining crust, roll out and create lattice strips. Place on top of filling. Brush lattice strips with egg wash. Bake for approximately 35 minutes, or until the lattice becomes golden brown.

Serve hot.

3 to 4 servings.

Dead Men's Bones

Ġhadam tal-Mejtin

This recipe, with a ghoulish name, actually is a sweet that was eaten on All Soul's Day, November 2.

Ingredients

4 egg whites
½ teaspoon cream of tartar
2/3 cup granulated sugar
1 teaspoon pure almond extract
2/3 cup freshly shelled almonds, ground

Method

Preheat the oven to 400° F.

With an electric or hand beater, whip the egg whites, cream of tartar, and sugar until stiff. Add almond extract. Stir in ground almonds and form into a dough. Chill. Place dough in a cookie press and shape like leg bones. Place on cookie sheet lined with parchment or rice paper. Bake for approximately 10 to 15 minutes, or until the bones turn golden brown.

Serve either hot or cold.

Makes approximately 18 small bones.

St. Martin's Cake

Kejk ta' San Martin

This is a traditional cake usually prepared for St. Martin's Day, November 11, although many families will make it at other times, too.

Ingredients

1 stick unsalted butter
½ cup granulated sugar
4 eggs, well beaten
1 cup all-purpose unbleached flour, sifted
½ cup orange juice
1 teaspoon mixed spice
¾ cup freshly shelled walnuts ,chopped
¾ cup freshly shelled hazelnuts, chopped
½ cup freshly shelled almonds, chopped
½ cup dried figs, chopped and soaked in orange juice or milk for 30 minutes to soften, or fig filling

Method

Preheat the oven to 350°F.

Using an electric beater, cream the butter and sugar. Fold in the eggs. Add flour, orange juice, mixed spice, walnuts, hazelnuts, almonds, and figs. Mix thoroughly. Carefully spoon mixture into a well-greased cake tin. Bake for approximately 60 to 90 minutes, or until a cake tester or a toothpick inserted in the enter of the cake comes out clean. Cool cake on a wire rack.

Serve cold.

6 to 8 servings.

Variations

Chopped dates that have been soaked in milk or orange juice can be substituted for the figs.

Treacle Rings

Qagħaq tal-Għasel

Now available year round in bakeries, treacle rings were associated with the feast of St. Martin, which falls in November. They also are served during Christmas. This dessert takes practice to make, but it is well worth it! This recipe is adapted from Gemma and Esther Said, owners of Gesters Restaurant, in Xaghra, Gozo.

Ingredients

For the pastry:

2 cups all-purpose unbleached flour, sifted
1 tablespoon sugar
1 stick margarine, softened
sufficient ice water to make dough

For the filling:

1¾ cup black treacle
1¾ cups granulated sugar
1 tablespoon unsweetened cocoa
2 tablespoons anisette liqueur
zest of orange rind
zest of lemon rind
½ teaspoon mixed spice
1¾ cups semolina

Method

For the pastry:

Mix flour and sugar. Cut in softened margarine with a pastry blender. Add water and roll dough into two balls. Wrap tightly in wax paper and refrigerate overnight.

For the filling:

Mix all the filling ingredients except the semolina in a sauce pan and bring to a boil. Add the semolina and reduce heat. Simmer until the mixture thickens enough for a spoon to stand upright in it. Let cool.

Roll out pastry in two rectangular strips. Place filling in middle of each strip. Roll pastry over the filling and join end-to-end to form two rings. Places slits in the pastry. Put rings on rice or parchment paper and bake until golden brown, approximately 40 minutes.

Serve at room temperature.

4 to 6 servings.

Kitchen Notes

These rings store well in closed tins.

Christmas Nut Ring

Qagħqa tal-Kavatelli

Ingredients

For the pastry:

2 cups all-purpose, unbleached flour, sifted
1 egg yolk
2 tablespoons sugar
8 ounces unsalted butter or margarine
½ cup unsweetened orange juice
1 shot glass anisette liqueur or 1 teaspoon anisette extract

For the syrup:

1 cup black treacle
rinds of one lemon, orange, and tangerine
3 ounces freshly shelled hazelnuts, chopped
3 ounces, freshly shelled almonds, chopped

Method

Preheat the oven to 375°F.

For the pastry:

In a large bowl, mix flour, egg yolk, and sugar. Cut in unsalted butter or margarine with a pastry blender. Add orange juice and anisette. Form dough into a ball. Cover with plastic wrap and refrigerate for at least one hour. Roll out dough as thin as possible, and cut into squares. Bake in a well-greased, floured cookie sheet for approximately 20 minutes, or until the pastry is golden brown.

For the syrup:

In a saucepot, simmer treacle and citrus rinds for approximately 15 minutes. Cool and set aside. Carefully place nuts and cooked pastry squares into the treacle mixture and then transfer to a large platter and arrange in a circle.

Serve at room temperature.

4 to 6 servings.

Kitchen Notes

Some Maltese families deep fry this dough instead of baking it.

Appendix

Many Maltese recipes call for stock or special doughs. For your convenience, I have placed these recipes here.

Vegetable Stock

Stokk tal-Ħaxix

Ingredients

2 large onions, peeled and chopped
2 cloves garlic, peeled and chopped
2 tablespoons olive or other vegetable oil
24 cups cold water
3 carrots, peeled and sliced
3 stalks celery, chopped
3 large ripe tomatoes, chopped or 1 can (28 ounces) peeled tomatoes or purée
2 teaspoons fresh peppercorns
4 to 6 sprigs Italian parsley, chopped
2 bay leaves
salt

Method

In large stockpot, sauté onion and garlic in olive oil until the onion becomes translucent, usually between 5 and 10 minutes. Add water and bring to a fast boil. Reduce heat. Add carrots, celery, tomatoes, fresh peppercorns, parsley, and bay leaves. Simmer for approximately one hour, until all vegetables are soft. Remove bay leaf and discard. Remove vegetables and serve as a separate dish.

For stock:

Cool. Using a fine-gauge metal mesh sieve, pour off remaining liquid. Ladle into 8-ounce cups or containers. Cover. Refrigerate for use within two days or freeze for future use. Add salt to taste before use.

Makes approximately 15 cups.

Chicken Stock

Stokk tat-Tiġieġ

Ingredients

2 large onions, peeled and chopped
2 to 3 cloves garlic, peeled and chopped
2 tablespoons olive or other vegetable oil
3 to 4 pounds of chicken backs and necks, rinsed under running cold water
1 to 2 medium size leeks, washed and chopped
4 large carrots, peeled and chopped
4 stalks celery, chopped
large handful of Italian parsley
2 tablespoons fresh peppercorns
2 to 3 sprigs thyme
2 bay leaves
24 cups cold water
salt

Method

In large stockpot, sauté chopped onion and garlic in olive oil until the onion become translucent, usually between 5 and 10 minutes. Add chicken necks and backs, leeks, carrots, celery, parsley, peppercorns, thyme, and bay leaves. Cover with water and bring to a boil. Then, simmer at least 2 hours, making certain chicken is well cooked. Carefully remove necks and backs, making certain no bones are left in the soup. Remove bay leaf and vegetables and discard.

For stock:

Gently pour off liquid into a large bowl and refrigerate for at least five hours or until the fat rises to the top, congeals, and can be skimmed off easily. Using a a fine-gauge metal mesh sieve, pour off remaining liquid. Ladle into 8 ounce cups or containers. Cover. Refrigerate for use within two days or freeze for future use. Add salt to taste before use.

Makes approximately 15 cups.

Beef Stock

Stokk taċ-Ċanga

Ingredients

3 large onions, peeled and chopped
2 to 3 cloves garlic, peeled and chopped
2 tablespoons olive or other vegetable oil
24 cups cold water
3 to 5 pounds beef bones without marrow
3 carrots, peeled, and sliced
3 stalks celery, chopped
3 large ripe tomatoes, chopped or 1 can (28 ounces) peeled or crushed tomatoes
2 tablespoons tomato paste
2 teaspoons fresh peppercorns
large handful of Italian parsley sprigs
2 bay leaves
salt to taste

Method

In large stockpot, sauté onions and garlic in olive oil until the onion becomes translucent, usually between 5 and 10 minutes. Add water and bring to a fast boil. Reduce heat. Add beef bones, carrots, celery, tomatoes, tomato paste, fresh peppercorns, parsley, and bay leaves. Simmer for approximately one hour, until all vegetables are soft. Remove beef bones, bay leaf, and vegetables and discard.

For stock: Cool. Skim off excess fat. Using a fine-gauge metal mesh sieve, pour off remaining liquid. Season to taste with salt. Ladle into 8-ounce cups or containers. Cover. Refrigerate for use within two days or freeze for future use. Add salt to taste before use.

Makes approximately 15 cups.

Kitchen Notes

Ask the butcher about the availability of beef bones. Don't neglect the butcher in the supermarket, who also might put aside and sell beef bones to customers who ask for them. Before they are used for making stock, beef bones should be roasted in a 350°F oven for approximately 30 minutes and then cooled.

If you prefer, use one to two pounds of beef shin. When the shin is cooked, it can be removed from the stock and eaten as part of a separate meal.

Fish Stock

Stokk Tal-Ħut

Ingredients

2 large onions, peeled and chopped
3 to 4 shallots, peeled and chopped
1 to 2 cloves garlic, peeled and chopped
2 tablespoons olive or other vegetable oil
2 large carrots, peeled and sliced
2 large stalks celery, chopped
large handful of Italian parsley, chopped
2 tablespoons fresh peppercorns
2 bay leaves
3 to 4 sprigs fresh thyme
lemon zest
1 to 2 sprigs fresh dill
24 cups cold water
4 to 5 pounds available fresh fish heads and bones, well rinsed
salt

Method

In a large stockpot, sauté onions, shallots, and garlic in olive oil until the onions and shallots become translucent, approximately 5 to 10 minutes. Add carrots, celery, parsley, peppercorns, bay leaves, thyme, lemon zest, and dill. Cover with water. Either place fish heads and bones in strainer and dunk into the stockpot or wrap them in muslin and simmer for approximately 1½ hours. Remove fish and discard. Vegetables may be discarded or served with another meal. Add salt to taste.

For stock: Cool. Using a fine-gauge metal mesh sieve, pour off remaining liquid. Ladle into 8-ounce cups or containers. Cover. Refrigerate for use within two days or freeze for future use. Add salt to taste before use.

Makes approximately 15 cups.

Basic Pastry Dough

Ingredients

4 cups all-purpose unbleached flour, sifted
½ teaspoon salt
12 tablespoons (1½ sticks) unsalted butter or margarine
12 tablespoons (¾ cup) vegetable shortening (lard may be substituted)
½ to ⅔ cups ice water

Method

In a large bowl, sift together flour and salt. Cut in butter and shortening with a pastry blender until the texture resembles coarse cornmeal. Drip in ice water, and form dough into two balls. Wrap each ball in plastic wrap or cover with a tea cloth and refrigerate for between one and two hours before rolling out. This dough can be frozen and used at a later time.

When rolling out dough, use a well-floured, hard (a marble board is an excellent investment) surface.

Yield:

Dough sufficient for a two-crust 9 inch pie.

Kitchen Notes

Although using ceramic or metal weights placed over wax paper can help prevent shrinking during pre-baking of the bottom crust, the use of aluminum foil also is recommended. Several kitchen specialty stores and mail-order companies have products that can eliminate the need for ceramic or metal weights.

Pastry Dough for Qassatat 1

Ingredients

2½ pounds (8 cups) all-purpose unbleached flour, sifted
1 tablespoon baking powder
1 teaspoon salt
2 sticks margarine
ice water for binding (approximately ½ to ⅔ cups)

Method

In a large bowl, sift together flour, baking powder, and salt. Cut in margarine until the flour resembles coarse cornmeal. Slowly add ice water until the flour can be formed into a large ball. Divide in two. Wrap each ball tightly in plastic wrap or cover bowl securely with a tea cloth. Refrigerate for at least 1 hour before using the dough for a recipe.

Makes approximately 12 to 15, 3-inch diameter *qassatat.*

Kitchen Notes

The dough, wrapped tightly in plastic, can be frozen and thawed when ready to be rolled out.

Pastry Dough for Qassatat 2

Ingredients

2½ pounds (8 cups) all-purpose unbleached flour, sifted
1 teaspoon salt
1 stick unsalted margarine
8 tablespoons vegetable shortening or lard
ice water for binding (approximately ½ to $^{2}/_{3}$ cups)

Method

In a large bowl, sift together flour and salt. Cut in margarine and shortening until the flour resembles coarse cornmeal. Gently add ice water until the flour can be formed into a large ball. Divide in two. Wrap each ball tightly in plastic wrap or cover bowl securely with a tea cloth. Refrigerate for at least 1 hour before working the dough for a recipe.

Makes approximately 12 to 15, 3-inch diameter *qassatat.*

Puff Pastry Dough (for pastizzi)

This is Wilfred Camilleri's recipe.

Ingredients

8 ounces all-purpose, unbleached flour, sifted
dash of salt
12 tablespoons (1½ sticks) margarine or unsalted butter (vegetable shortening is used by many people)
6 to 7 tablespoons ice water

Method

Sift flour and salt together. Divide the margarine into half-inch squares. Drop margarine squares into flour making sure not to squish them. Mix lightly until all margarine cubes are covered with flour (make sure that the cubes remain intact.) Add water and mix lightly with a knife, again making sure that the cubes remain intact. If some flour is left loose, add a teaspoon of cold water at a time until all the flour is used. The resulting dough should be very soft.

Sprinkle flour on the dough and the working surface. Gently roll the dough into an elongated shape.

Sprinkle flour on the rolling pin and roll the dough until it is approximately 8 inches long and not more than 5 inches wide. Now do the steps below exactly.

1. Fold the lower third toward the top. Then, fold the upper third toward the bottom on top of the first fold. You should end up with a three-layered rectangle. With light pressure from the rolling pin, seal the three edges.

2. Remove extra flour. Turn the folded dough counter-clockwise so that the right side is at the top. Roll the dough lightly until it is 9 inches long and 6 inches wide.

3. Repeat steps 1 and 2.

4. Cover the dough with a damp cloth and store in the refrigerator for approximately 30 minutes.

5. Repeat steps 1 through 4, four times.

The dough can now be rolled out to the desired thickness.

Kitchen Notes

Here are a few of Wilfred's " kitchen secrets."

"Keep everything cold. The dough must also be kept cold at all times. The best working surface for the dough is a slab of marble since marble tends to stay cool. Always store the dough covered with a damp cloth in your refrigerator, but before storing it, make sure you remove any loose flour. Always sprinkle the working surface, the rolling pin, and the dough with flour before you start working the dough. Never turn over the dough while you are working it. Instead, turn it flat on the board (or turn the board itself) clockwise before each rolling and always in the same direction. This is one of the most difficult doughs to make, and you may have to try it a few times before you get it right!"

Make no mistake. This dough takes practice to master. . . but your first attempts will taste good nevertheless! Even "mistakes"—remember my Nanna Glaudina and hers—are worth the effort!

What Did You Say?

Mfejjaq. Tiftaħar. Għasel iswed.*

No, the typesetter is not having a bad day and your eyes are not playing tricks on you.

What you will see on signs and hear in conversations while in Malta is *Malti*, a Semitic language based on the Latin alphabet that has emerged from the island's long history of visitors.

Linguists believe the roots of *Malti*, date to the ancient Phoenicians, who made Malta their home. And there have been strong influences from the semitic languages Hebrew, Amharic, and Arabic. Maltese is the only Semitic language officially written in the Latin alphabet. Linguists say that modern Maltese vernacular is closely related to the western Arabic dialects. In its phonetics, morphology, syntax, and vocabulary it shows the strong influence of an earlier, later, and continuing Sicilian (Latin) form of speech.

There are 29 letters, excluding the letter "y," in the Maltese alphabet. It is believed that years of Arab domination contributed to the Semitic structure of the language, but other occupations and influences—Norman, Spanish, Italian, French, British, and even the presence of the Knights of St. John—also have played a crucial role in the evolution of the Maltese language.

Some examples: *Alla* is "God" in Maltese and in Arabic. "Thank you "—*grazzi*—is similar to the Italian word "grazie;" *dixx* is like the English word "dish"; and *xabo* is like the French word "jabot" or the frill of a shirt.

Not surprisingly, Maltese children learn several languages in school—Malti, English, Italian, Spanish, French, and Arabic, starting in the first grade. Many will tell you that they find English much easier to learn, write, and speak than their native Malti.

*For the curious; *Mfejjaq* means "cured"; *tifiahar*, "to brag;" and *ghasel iswed* is dark honey.

Resources

The Malta Bakery (JMJ International Baking Corp.)
23-02 38th Ave.
Long Island City, N.Y. 11101
(718) 392-7280; Fax (718) 392-9674

In addition to *pastizzi,* Malta Bakery sells Maltese specialties such as *qassatat, qaghaq tal-ghasel, biskuttelli, timpana,* and *ross fil-forn.* They also make crusty Maltese bread and *ftira,* a semi-leavened flat bread with a hole in its center. Also provides mail-order and catering services.

Malta Bake Shop
3256 Dundas St., West
Toronto, Ontario, Canada M6P 2A3
(416) 769-2174
E-mail: maltabak@globalserve.net

Sells cooked or frozen *pastizzi* and *qassatat,* as well as, *fenkata, gbejniet bil-zar, galleti, qaghag tal-ghasel, biskutelli, qaghag-gulglien, pastini tal-lewz,* and the Maltese soft drink *Kinnie* at the shop and restaurant. Mail-order of most goods to Canada and the United States is available.

Basket Bakery
240 Clarence St.
Brampton, Ontario, Canada L6W 1T4
(905) 457-2732

Sells Maltese specialty items such as *pastizzi* and *qassatat.*

Basket Bakery
50 Kennedy Road South
Brampton, Ontario, Canada L6W 1T4
(905) 457-2738

Sells Maltese specialty items such as *pastizzi,* and *qassatat.*

TASTE OF MALTA

Buskett Bakery
3029 Dundas St., West
Toronto, Ontario, Canada M6T 1Z4
(416) 763-2562

Sells Maltese specialty items such as *pastizzi* and *qassatat.*

Valletta Bakery
3082 Dundas St., West
Toronto, Ontario, Canada M6P 1Z8
(416) 762-0702

Sells Maltese specialties such as *pastizzi* and *qassatat.*

Joe's *pastizzi* Plus
5070 Dundas St., West
Toronto, Ontario, Canada M9A 1B9
(416) 233-9063

Sells fresh or frozen *pastizzi* and other Maltese specialties such as *qassatat, ravioli*, and *timpana.* Restaurant service also is available.

D'Artagnan
399 St. Paul Ave.
Jersey City, N. J. 07306
(800) DAR-TAGN; Fax (201) 792-0748

Sells fresh killed rabbits, other fine meats, and escargots by mail-order.

Joie de Vivre
P. O. Box 875
Modesto, Calif. 95353
(800) 648-8854; Fax (209) 869-0788

Sells fresh killed rabbits, guinea fowl, and other specialties by mail-order.

New England Cheesemaking Supply Co.
P.O. Box 85
Main St.
Ashfield, Mass. 01330-0085
(413) 628-3801; Fax (413) 628-4061
E-mail: info@cheesemaking.com
http//www.cheesemaking.com

Sells cheesemaking supplies, such as rennets and molds, for individuals who want to make cheeses, such as *gbejneit*, at home.

Indo-European Foods, Inc.
1000 Air Way
Glendale, Calif. 91201
(213) 722-2100; Fax (818) 247-9722

Sells an extensive variety of Mediterranean foods such as broad beans, orange flower water, and mixed spice by mail-order.

Mozzarella Co.
2944 Elm St.
Dallas, Texas 75226
(800) 798-2954; Fax (214) 7241-4076
MozzCo@aol.com

Sells fresh mozzarella, ricotta, and other cheeses by mail-order direct from the factory.

B & L Specialty Foods
P.O. Box 80068
Seattle, Wash. 98108-0068
(800) Eat Pasta
http://www.blfooods.com/

Sells specialty cheeses and flours, dried beans including favas, fruits, chestnut purée, fish, and canned anchovies through mail-order.

Penzey's Spice House
1921 S. West Ave.
Waukesha, Wis. 53186
(414) 574-0277

Sells hard-to-find ingredients like orange and rose flower waters unusual spices, and special spice blends for sausage at their retail store and through mail-order.

Falcon Beverage Services Ltd.
240 Clarence St.
Brampton, Ontario, Canada L6W 1T4
(905) 457-2732

Distributes the soft drink *Kinnie* in Canada. Check for availability in the United States.

The British Pepper and Spice Co., Ltd.
Rholi Road Brackmills
Northampton, NN4 OLD England

Manufactures and exports the Millstone brand of mixed spice. Check for availability in the United States and Canada.

Goya Foods, Inc.
1000 Seaview Drive
Secaucus, N.J. 07096
(201) 348-4900

Sells a variety of dried beans such as favas, as well as imported olives and capers, which usually are available in larger supermarket or ethnic groceries.

Mediterranean Foods
30-12 34th St.
Astoria, N.Y. 11103
(718) 728-6166

Sells specialty items, including spices, through mail-order.

The Spice House
1941 Central St.
Evanston, IL. 60201
(847) 328-3711 Fax: (847) 328-3631
Sells specialty spices through mail-order.

The British Gourmet Chandlers
45 Wall St.
Madison, Conn. 06443
(800) 8GB-NOSH; (203) 245-4521; Fax: (203) 245-3477
http://www.thebritishshoppe.com
Sells British specialty products through mail-order, including treacle and Lyons brand mixed spice, which is not listed in their catalog but is available on request.

King Arthur Flour Co.
P.O. Box 876
Norwich, Vt. 05055-0876
(800) 827-6836
Sells specialty American and European flours, spices, candied fruits and peels, flower waters, and quality, hard-to-find baking equipment such as the Pie Partner, which can be used for pre-baking pie crusts, by mail-order.

Williams-Sonoma
P.O. Box 7456
San Francisco, Calif. 94120-7456
(800) 541-2233
Sells quality cooking equipment and supplies such as artichoke and other vegetable steamers plus specialty items.

Sur La Table: Tools for the Cook
1765 Sixth Ave., South
Seattle, Wash. 98134-1608
(800) 243-0852
Sells hard-to-find quality cooking supplies such as herb shredders and mincers by mail-order.

Bridge Kitchenware, Inc.
214 E. 52nd St.
New York, N.Y. 10022
(212) 688-4220; (800) 274-3435) for ordering through their catalog.

Sells professional and hard-to-find cooking supplies such as large animal cutters, which can be used to create *figolli*, and multi-sized biscuit cutters useful for making *pastizzi* and *qassatat*.

Sadson Ltd.
54 St. Francis Square
Qormi, Malta
011 356 487 325; Fax 011 356 419 031
E-mail: sadson@global.net.mt

Manufactures and exports the Maltese liqueur, *Tamakari*. Check for availability in the United States and Canada.

Master Wine Ltd.
Oratory St.
Naxxar, Malta
011 356 412391; fax 011 356 437129

Manufactures and exports the Maltese liqueur *Madlien*. Check for availability in the United States and Canada.

Hamrun Dairy Products, Ltd.
The Dairy
Old Railway Station
Hamrun HMR 08 Malta

Manufactures and distributes cheeses such as *gbejniet tal-bzar* throughout Malta. Check for availability of *gbejniet tal-bzar* in the United States and Canada.

The Gilway Co., Ltd.
17 Arcadian Ave.
Paramus, N.J. 07652
(201) 843-8152; Fax (201) 843-8221

Imports from England one-pound cans of Lyles black treacle and Lyles golden syrup and provides mail-order service in the United States and Canada.

Cultural and Professional Associations

Maltese Center
27-20 Hoyt Ave., South
Astoria, N.Y. 11102
(718) 728-9883; Fax (718) 784-2237

Holds various cultural events; sells freshly made and frozen *pastizzi* on weekends. Call for program information and hours.

Maltese-American Benevolent Society, Inc.
1832 Michigan Ave.
Detroit, Mich. 48216
(313) 961-8393

Holds various cultural events; sells freshly made and frozen *pastizzi*. Call for program information and hours.

Maltese-American Community Club
5221 Oakman Blvd.
Dearborn, Mich. 48126
(313) 846-7077

Holds various cultural events; sells freshly made and frozen *pastizzi*. Call for program information and hours.

Maltese-American Social Club of San Francisco, Inc.
924 El Camino Reale
South San Francisco, Calif. 94080
(650) 871-4611

Holds various cultural events. Call for program information and hours.

St. Elizabeth's-Maltese Society
449 Holyoke St.
San Francisco, Calif. 94134
(415) 468-0820

Holds various cultural events. Call for program information.

Maltese Cultural Association
2938 Dundas St., West
P. O. Box 70587
Toronto, Ontario, Canada M6P 4E7
(905) 276-1734

Publishes *Wirt Malta*, a quarterly cultural and news magazine for the Maltese communities in Canada and the United States. Holds various cultural events. Call for program information and hours.

Maltese Canadian Club
70 Charterhouse Crescent
London, Ontario, Canada M5W 5C5
(519) 451-8563

Maltese-Canadian Society of Toronto
235 Medlan Ave.
Toronto, Ontario, Canada M6P 2N6
(416) 767-3645

Maltese-Canadian Professional and Business Association
3300 Bloor St., West
West Tower, Suite 625
Etobicoke, Ontario, Canada M8X 2X2
(416) 234-2265; Fax: (416) 234-2281

This organization promotes professional, economic, business, and cultural relations between Malta and Canada.

Malta Band Club, Inc.
5745 Coopers Ave.
Mississauga, Ontario, Canada L4Z 1R9
(905) 890-8507

This is an active Canadian organization promoting Maltese culture in Canada. They publish a monthly newsletter.

St. Paul The Apostle Roman Catholic Church
3224 Dundas St., West
Toronto, Ontario, Canada M6P 2A3
(416) 767-7054

This is the church of the Maltese community in Toronto. Several masses a week are held in Maltese. This church also sponsors religious events for the Maltese country.

San Gorg Festa Association
3029 Dundas St., West
Toronto, Ontario, Canada M6T 1Z4
(416) 763-2562

This group organizes an annual supper dinner/dance, usually in early May for the feast of San Gorg.

Gozo Club
3265 Dundas St., West
Toronto, Ontario, Canada M6P 2AP
(416) 233-9063

Promotes Gozitan culture.

Melita Soccer Club
3336 Dundas St., West
Toronto, Ontario, Canada M6P 2AP
(416) 763-5317

Promotes Maltese soccer and other sports.

Organizations Outside of North America

Deutsche-Maltesische Gesellschaft (Maltese-German Association)
Mittelbachstrasse 26
53518 Adenau, Germany
011 49 02 691 501; Fax 011 49 02 691 2283

Sponsors youth and cultural exchange programs between Malta and Germany. The organization publishes a quarterly newsletter for members.

Associazione Napoletana Amici di Malta
Via Ponte di Tappia 82
80133 Naples, Italy
011 39 321-573; 2341453

Publishes *Malta Napoli - Corriere Mediterraneo.*

Association France Malte
60 rue de la Chapelle
75018 Paris, France
011 33 1 42 40 44 27

Association les Amis de Malte
13 rue Paul Meriel
64000 Toulouse, France

Centre Culturel-les Amis de Malte
7 allee du Perolier
69130 Ecully, France

Malta-Geneva Association
6, chemin Gustave-Rochette
CH-1213 Onex, Switzerland
P. L. Bonferroni, President
011 41 22 792 60 37; Fax 011 41 24 492 13 81
E-mail: 100443.3264@compuserve.com

Promotes cultural and business contacts and exchanges between Geneva and Malta.

Maltese Federal Council of Australia
c/o Maltese Community Council of South Australia
P.O. Box 16
Woodville, 5011 South Australia

This organization represents the Maltese communities on matters of national interest with the Australian and Maltese governments.

La Valette Social Centre
175 Walters Road
Blacktown, NSW
2148 Australia
011 61 622 5847; Fax: 011 61 831 2722

Sponsors Maltese folk singing, and serves Maltese cuisine on Saturday nights. Publishes the annual Maltese Resource Directory, describing topics of interest to Maltese-Australians in New South Wales, Western Australia, South Australia, Queensland, and Tasmania.

Maltese-Australian Business and Professional Association
c/o16 Donald St.
Yennora, NSW
2161 Australia
011 61 892 1777; Fax 011 61 516 3006

Promotes business, culture, and commerce between the two countries.

Maltese Cultural Association of New South Wales
c/o 5 Calla Grove
Pendle Hill NSW
2145 Australia
011 61 631 0989

Organizes Maltese cultural shows, displays, music, singing, folk dancing, and Maltese language classes. It celebrates the traditional Festa of St Paul on June 7th.

Maltese Australian Women's Association
c/o 75 Floss St.
Hurlstone Park NSW 2193 Australia
011 61 558 6102

Sponsors social, recreational, and educational activities.

Association of Maltese Communities of Egypt (AMCE),
incorporating The Friends of Malta G.C.
14 Cheviot Close
Enfield, Middlesex EN1 3UY
United Kingdom

The AMCE publishes a semi-annual newsletter.

The Malta League
21 Oaklea
Welwyn, Hertfordshire AL6 0PT
United Kingdom

Finnish-Maltese Society (Suomi-Malta Seura)
Poste Restante 00300
Helsinki, Finland
Sakari Warseell, Chairman
Edward Iles, Vice-President
011 358 9 340 2304

This organization arranges Maltese cultural programs and publishes a semi-annual magazine, *Maltaset.*

Publications of Interest Published Outside of Malta

Pauline Acquilina, Managing Editor
Wirt Malta, The Legacy of Malta
Maltese Cultural Association of Canada
2938 Dundas St., West
Box 70587
Toronto, Ontario, Canada M6P 4E7
(905) 276-1734

George Mallia, Editor
L-Ahbar — Il Gazzetta ghall-Maltin tal-Kanada
2336 Bloor St., West
Box 84554
Toronto, Ontario, Canada M6S 4Z7

This is a bi-language monthly newspaper publishing news and feature articles about Malta as well as columns and book reviews.

Lino Vella, Managing Editor
The Maltese Herald
195 Merrylands Road
Merrylands, NSW 2160 Australia
011 61 9637 9992; Fax 011 61 9682 1923

Written in both Maltese and English, this is the only national Maltese newspaper in Australia.

Information about Malta

Malta National Tourist Office
Michael Piscopo, Director
350 Fifth Ave., Suite 4412
New York, N.Y. 10118
(212) 695-9520; Fax: (212) 695-8229
E-mail: office.us@tourism.org.mt
http://www.visitmalta.com

Consulate General of Malta
3300 Bloor St., West
Etobiocoke, Ontario, Canada M8X 2X2
(416) 207-0922; fax (416) 207-0986

Malta National Tourist Office
280 Republic St.
Valletta CMR 02, Malta
011 356 22 44 44/5, 22 50 48/9; Fax: 011 356 22 04 01
E-mail: info@tourism.org.mt
http://www.visitmalta.com

Malta National Tourist Office
Malta House
36-38 Piccadilly
London WIV 0PP, England
011 44 0 171 292-4900; Fax: 011 44 0 171 734-1880

National Verkeersbureau, Malta
Geelvinck Gebouw 4e
Singel 540
1017 AZ Amsterdam, The Netherlands
011 31 20 620-7223; Fax: 011 31 20 620-7233

Office du Tourisme de Malte
9 Cite de Trevise, 75009 Paris, France
011 33 1 48 00 03 79; Fax: 011 33 1 48 00 04 41

Fremdenverkehrsamt Malta
Schillerstrasse 30-4
D-60313 Frankfurt am Main, Germany
011 49 69 28 58 90/ 49 69 2 07 88; Fax: 011 49 69 28 54 79

Ente Nazionale per il Turismo di Malta
Via Larga 7
20122 Milan, Italy
011 39 02 58 30 75 59; Fax: 011 39 02 58 30 70 29

World Wide Web Sources

Grazio's Malta Virtualwali
http://www.fred.net.malta/

Maintained by Dr. Grazio Falzon, this netsource provides an extensive listing — up-dated frequently — of Maltese facts, cuisine, history, folklore, archeology, politics, literature, and culture.

Malta — A Jewel in the Mediterranean
http://web.idirect.com/~malta

This is an extensive netsource of Maltese facts, history, cuisine, and a calendar of events for various Maltese organizations in Canada maintained by Wilfred Camilleri.

Joe Farrugia's Malta and Gozo — Island in the Sun
http://www.geocities.com/TheTropics/2767

The home page of United Kingdom-based Joe Farrugia focuses on Maltese history, services, and culture.

Search Malta
http://www.searchmalta.com

Maintained by Antoine Zammit, this search engine has an index of information about Maltese services, companies, culture, food, and restaurants and hotels in Malta.

Resources

Malta Internet Group

Members of this internet list-serve discuss Maltese politics, culture, history, and sometimes, cuisine. To subscribe: send an E-mail message to majordomo@angus.mystery. com. In the message section, type: "subscribe Malta."

It's Malta
http://www.visitmalta.com

A web site about Malta hosted by the Malta National Tourism organization.

Bibliography

Mary and Peter Bellizzi, *Health at the Maltese Table*, Klabb Kotba Maltin, Valletta, Malta, 1992.

Carmen Carbonaro, Maltese Dishes, Veritas Press, 5th ed., Zabbar, Malta, 1971.

Paul Cassar, M.D., *Early Relations Between Malta and U.S.A.*, Midsea Books, Valletta, Malta, 1976.

Michael Diacono, "Il-kcina Maltija," in *Il-Gens*, November 1, 1991, pp. 12-13.

Anton B. Dougall, *Anton Dougall's Taste of Malta*, Klabb Tat-Tisjir, Valletta, Malta, 1993.

Anton B. Dougall, *Lampuki u Hut Iehor* (*Lampuki and Other Fish*), Klabb Tat-Tisjir, Valletta, Malta, 1989.

Anton B. Dougall, *Kcina Maltija (Maltese Kitchen)*, Union Press, Valletta, Malta, 1974.

Anton B. Dougall, *Helu* (*Sweets*), Klabb Tat-Tisjir, Valletta, Malta, 1990.

"Drawwiet ta'ikel f'Malta," in *Il-Gens*, July 16, 1996, pp. 12-13.

Anne and Helen Caruana Galizia, *Recipes from Malta: A Guide to*

Traditional Maltese Cookery, Progress Press Co., Ltd., Valletta, 1972.

Sharon Tyler Herbst, *Food Lover's Companion*, 2nd. ed., Barrons Cooking Guide, Hauppauge, N.Y., 1995.

Pamela Parkinson-Lange, *A Taste of Malta — The Food of the Knights of Malta*, MAG Publications, Lija, Malta, 1995.

Malta Ministry of Tourism, *Handbook for Tourist Guides*, Floriana, Malta, January, 1975.

Marie L. Pickering, *Simplified Cooking including Maltese Recipes*, Midsea Books Ltd., Valletta, Malta, 1975.

Plurigraf Publishers, *The Best of Maltese Cooking*, Narni, Italy, 1994.

Guze Cassar Pullicino, "Antichi Cibi Maltesi," in *Melita Historica*, Vol. 2, No. 2, pp. 31-54, 1961.

Guze Cassar Pullicino, "Foreign Influence on Maltese Cooking: A Review of Traditions and Customs," in *The Sunday Times of Malta*, December 17, 1961, p. 11.

Lola Sammut, "Maltese Cookery," in *The Malta Yearbook 1976*, De La Salle Brothers Publications, Sliema, Malta, pp. 389-397, 1976.

Lola Sammut, "A Calendar of Maltese Food," in *The Malta Yearbook, 1977*, De La Salle Brothers Publications, Sliema, Malta, pp. 449-455, 1977.

Jenny Scicluna and Pippa Mattei, compilers, *Specialties from Malta for Your Table*, Round Table, Malta, undated.

Valerie, Cooking — *Maltese Cuisine*, Publishers Enterprises Group, Ltd., Marsa, Malta, 1990.

Bibliography

Valerie, Tisjir 1, *Ricetti Varjati minn Valerie,* Gulf Publishing, Ltd., Valletta, Malta, 1980.

Valerie, Tisjir 2, *Ricetti Maltin minn Valerie,* Gulf Publishing, Ltd., Valletta, Malta, 1981.

Valerie, Tisjir 3, *Ricetti Tal-helu minn Valerie,* Gulf Publishing, Ltd., Valletta, Malta, 1981.

Louis Zammit, M.D., *An Atlas of Mediterranean Fish,* privately printed, Malta, 1991.

Index

Index

Also from Hippocrene . . .

MALTESE-ENGLISH/ENGLISH-MALTESE DICTIONARY & PHRASEBOOK

Grazio Falzon

Written especially for Americans, this handy new dictionary and lexically-grouped phrasebook is an ideal companion for travelers.

- 1,500 entries
- Introduction to basic grammar
- Pronunciation guide
- Maltese-English/English-Maltese dictionary
- Maltese phrasebook, including all topics a visitor to Malta needs to know
- A must for anyone traveling to the Republic of Malta

155 pages • 3 ¾ x 7 • 1,500 entries • 0-7818-0565-1 • $11.95pb • (697)

TRADITIONAL SOUTH AFRICAN COOKERY

Hildegonda Duckitt

A collection of recipes culled from two previous books by the author, this volume provides ideas for tasty, British- and Dutch-inspired meals and insight into daily life of colonial Africa.

178 pages • 5 x 8 ½ • 0-7818-0490-6 • W • $10.95pb • (352)

THE JOY OF CHINESE COOKING

Doreen Yen Hung Feng

Includes over two hundred kitchen-tested recipes and a thorough index.

226 pages • 5 ½ x 7 ½ • illustrations • 0-7818-0097-8 • W • $8.95pb • (288)

EGYPTIAN COOKING

Samia Abdennour

Almost 400 recipes, all adapted for the North American kitchen, represent the best of authentic Egyptian family cooking.

199 pages • 5 ½ x 8 ½ • 0-7818-0643-7 • NA • $11.95pb • (727)

ART OF SOUTH INDIAN COOKING

Alamelu Vairavan and Patricia Marquardt

Over 100 recipes for tempting appetizers, chutneys, rice dishes, vegetables and stews—flavored with onions, tomatoes, garlic, and delicate spices in varying combinations¾have been adapted for the Western kitchen.

202 pages • 5 ½ x 8 ½ • 0-7818-0525-2 • W • $22.50 • (635)

BEST OF GOAN COOKING

Gilda Mendonsa

This book is a rare and authentic collection of over 130 of the finest Goan recipes and 12 pages of full color illustrations. From Goa—a region in Western India once colonized by the Portuguese—comes a cuisine in which the hot, sour and spicy flavors mingle in delicate perfection, a reflection of the combination of Arabian, Portuguese and Indian cultures that have inhabited the region.

106 pages • 7 x 9 ¼ • 12 pages color illustrations • 0-7818-0584-8 • NA • $8.95pb • (682)

THE BEST OF KASHMIRI COOKING

Neerja Mattoo

With nearly 90 recipes and 12 pages of color photographs, this cookbook is a wonderful introduction to Kashmiri dishes, considered the height of gourmet Indian cuisine.

131 pages • 5 ½ x8 ½ • 12 pages color photographs • 0-7818-0612-7 • NA • $9.95pb • (724)

THE ART OF PERSIAN COOKING

Forough Hekmat

This collection of 200 recipes features such traditional Persian dishes as Abgushte Adas • (Lentil soup), Mosamme Khoreshe • (Eggplant Stew), Lamb Kebab, Cucumber Borani • (Special Cucumber Salad), Sugar Halva and Gol Moraba • (Flower Preserves).

190 pages • 5 ½ x 8 ½ • 0-7818-0241-5 • W • $9.95pb • (125)

THE ART OF ISRAELI COOKING

Chef Aldo Nahoum

All of the 250 recipes are kosher.

"[Includes] a host of new indigenous Israeli recipes with dishes that reflect the eclectic and colorful nature of Israeli cuisine." –Jewish Week

125 pages • 5 ½ x 8 ½ • 0-7818-0096-X • W • $9.95pb • (252)

THE ART OF TURKISH COOKING

Nesret Eren

"Her recipes are utterly mouthwatering, and I cannot remember a time when a book so inspired me to take pot in hand."—Nika Hazelton, The New York Times Book Review

308 pages • 5 ½ x 8 ½ • 0-7818-0201-6 • W • $12.95pb • (162)

THE HONEY COOKBOOK: RECIPES FOR HEALTHY LIVING

Maria Lo Pinto

Much more than a cookbook, this indispensable guide includes a variety of uses for honey. In addition to 240 recipes, the book features a section on complete menu suggestions, cooking tips, weights and measures, substitutions, glossary and index.

174 pages • 5 x 8 ½ • 0-7818-0149-4 • W • $8.95pb • (283)

COOKING THE CARIBBEAN WAY

Mary Slater

Here are 450 authentic Caribbean recipes adapted for the North American kitchen, including Bermuda Steamed Mussels, Port Royal Lamb Stew, and Mango Ice-cream.

256 pages • 5 ½ x 8 ½ • 0-7818-0638-0 • W • $11.95pb • (725)

MAYAN COOKING: CLASSIC RECIPES FROM THE SUN KINGDOMS OF MEXICO

Cherry Hamman

This unique cookbook contains not only 200 colorful and exotic recipes

from the Mexican Yucatan, but also the author's fascinating observations on a vanishing way of life.
250 pages • 5 ½ x8 ½ • 0-7818-0580-5 • W • $24.95hc • (680)

ART OF SOUTH AMERICAN COOKERY

Myra Waldo

This cookbook offers delicious recipes for the various courses of a typical South American meal. Dishes show the expected influence of Spanish and Portuguese cuisines, but are enhanced by the use of locally available ingredients.
266 pages • 5 x 8 ½ • b/w line drawings • 0-7818-0485-X • W • $11.95pb • (423)

THE ART OF BRAZILIAN COOKERY

Dolores Botafogo

Over three hundred savory and varied recipes fill this cookbook of authentic Brazilian cuisine, ranging from Churasco (barbecued steak) and Vatapa (Afro-Brazilian fish porridge from the Amazon) to sweets, and aromatic Brazilian coffees.
240 pages • 5 ½ x 8 ½ • 0-7818-0130-3 • W • $11.95pb • (250)

BAVARIAN COOKING

Olli Leeb

With over 300 recipes, this lovely collector's item cookbook covers every aspect of Bavarian cuisine from drinks, salads and breads to main courses and desserts. Includes a large fold-out map and cultural calendar along with 10 pages of color photographs.

"Bavarian Cooking *is what a good regional cookbook should be—a guide for those who wish to know the heart and soul of a region's cooking, a book that anchors its recipes in the culture that produced them, and a cookbook that brings delight to the casual reader as well as to the serious cook.*"
—German Life
171 pages • 6 ½ x 8 ¼ • line illustrations and 10 pages color photographs • 0-7818-0561-9 • NA • $25.00 • (659)

A BELGIAN COOKBOOK

Juliette Elkon

A celebration of the regional variations found in Belgian cuisine.
224 pages • 5 ½ x 8 ½ • 0-7818-0461-2 • W • $12.95pb • (535)

THE ART OF IRISH COOKING

Monica Sheridan

Nearly 200 recipes for traditional Irish fare.
166 pages • 5 ½ x 8 ½ • illustrated • 0-7818-0454-X • W • $12.95pb • (335)

CELTIC COOKBOOK: Traditional Recipes from the Six Celtic Lands Brittany, Cornwall, Ireland, Isle of Man, Scotland and Wales

Helen Smith-Twiddy

This collection of over 160 recipes from the Celtic world includes traditional, yet still popular dishes like *Rabbit Hoggan* and *Gwydd y Dolig* (Stuffed Goose in Red Wine).

200 pages • 5 ½ x 8 ½ • 0-7818-0579-1 • NA • $22.50hc • (679)

ENGLISH ROYAL COOKBOOK: FAVORITE COURT RECIPES

Elizabeth Craig

Dine like a King or Queen with this unique collection of over 350 favorite recipes of the English royals, spanning 500 years of feasts! Try recipes like Duke of York Consommé and Crown Jewel Cake, or even a Princess Mary Cocktail. Charmingly illustrated throughout.

187 pages • 5 ½ x 8 ½ • illustrations • 0-7818-0583-X • W • $11.95pb • (723)

TRADITIONAL RECIPES FROM OLD ENGLAND

Arranged by country, this charming classic features the favorite dishes and mealtime customs from across England, Scotland, Wales and Ireland.

110 pages • 5 x 8 ½ • illustrated • 0-7818-0489-2 • W • $9.95pb • (157)

ART OF DUTCH COOKING

C. Countess van Limburg Stirum

This attractive volume of 200 recipes offers a complete cross section of Dutch home cooking, adapted to American kitchens. A whole chapter is devoted to the Dutch Christmas, with recipes for unique cookies and candies that are a traditional part of the festivities.

192 pages • 5 ½ x 8 ½ • illustrations • 0-7818-0582-1 • W • $11.95pb • (683)